Full-time to Fulfilled

The blueprint to success as an independent consultant

Matt Crabtree

WWW.GET-KNOWN.CO.UK

To Rowena, Charlotte and Hannah.

Contents

This book is for...

Mid/late-career professionals who want more from their future than just another step up the ladder, either at the same organisation or even at a shiny new one.

It's for people for whom the fancy title, the place on the org chart, the big brand and all the other trappings and trinkets of full-time roles no longer hold any appeal.

It's for people who've seen other independent consultants operating and have thought 'I can do that', maybe even thought 'I can do that – a whole lot better'!

It's for people who've got a specialism for which they're well known and well regarded. They're not the best necessarily but at least better than average.

It's for people who want to call themselves consultants, coaches, advisors, mentors, trainers, speakers, facilitators, or even interim leaders. (It's not for freelance contractors who get their work through agencies/platforms though.)

It's for people who've spent their career so far building generally good relationships with colleagues and business partners and who don't have a trail of dead bodies behind them.

And it's for people who don't want to keep devoting the better part of their waking hours to a single organisation who might not always be as loyal in return.

Above all else, it's for people who believe there is more to life than work and want to find a way of staying actively engaged professionally but very much on their own terms.

This book will...

Show you exactly how to turn your experience into a sustainable, multi-six-figure independent consulting practice, without ever once having to cold call or spam email someone who doesn't know you.

It's packed full of practical and proven how-to guides that will support you from making the decision to become an independent consultant, to launching yourself to the world and all the way to winning and delivering your first engagements.

You'll hear stories of real people just like you who have made the step from a full-time role with a single organisation to multiple concurrent engagements with a range of clients and more freedom, fulfillment and security in their lives than they could ever have imagined.

You'll learn why so much of the well-meaning advice you'll be given by people who've never walked this path is horribly wrong and why so many of the books on this subject make better doorstops than guides to success.

It's the product of nearly two decades of trial and error and is written by someone who is a practising consultant and consistently bills more than £0.5m per year.

Meet Matt

Matt is:

▶ A farmer's son with a qualification in agriculture that is of questionable value

▶ A former senior leader in the telecoms, technology and financial services industries

▶ The founder of global consulting firm and Certified B Corporation®, Positive Momentum

▶ A passionate social and environmental activist and electric vehicle bore

▶ The (often overly) enthusiastic host of podcast series, Meet The CEO

▶ A Prince's Trust, Generation Success and Aleto Foundation mentor

▶ A former school governor

▶ An occasional half marathon runner who has no ambition to double that distance

- A grateful husband to the person who made all this happen

- A proud father to two remarkable young women.

Matt has:

- Achieved his first board level position (of a $0.5bn firm) by the age of just 29

- Worked with more than 1,000 different organisations, from Fortune 500s to startups

- Delivered speeches in every corner of the world to more than 750,000 delegates

- Helped countless other consultants to develop their own independent practices.

Looking closer:

- www.mattcrabtree.co.uk

- www.positivemomentum.com/meet-the-team/matt-crabtree

- www.linkedin.com/in/mattcrabtree

- @mattcrabtree

- @Pos_Mom

I wrote this book...

Because, when I first set out as an independent consultant, I wasted too much time going in the wrong direction and I'm frustrated seeing people making the same mistakes.

How to use this book

N one of this is meant to be passive – it can't be that. Nothing about the journey you have taken so far has been easy, so why would that change now? The next phase of your career will only be successful, enjoyable and sustained if you are well prepared and creative in your approach. But that needs a foundation, a real platform.

Beyond the advice and experience offered throughout this book, there's also a wide variety of free resources available to you from the Positive Momentum Network website. Using the free resources to really support the ideas explored in this book will help you to properly map out the process of taking yourself from your initial idea to its successful implementation and then on to growing and maximising your independent consultancy business. The resources are designed to help you get started, grow your network, win business and deliver effectively. To get started head to **www.positivemomentum.com/network** and sign up for free.

Part 1

20 Years of Trial and Error

CHAPTER 1

My Story

From Farmer to Consultant

I was born at the very end of the 1960s on a farm in the rural South Midlands of the UK – and about as far away from the life I lead today as it's possible to imagine.

Long summers were spent harvesting, with winters endured shivering in the dairy, but I loved every minute of it. Slightly too much as it turns out since my school reports were generally in the 'could do better' category.

Whilst I just about managed to get a place at agricultural college – which was as much of a social education than anything else – it was clear I was never really destined to spend the rest of my life down on the farm.

In actual fact, my father ran a large estate owned by an aristocratic family and so the farm I grew up on was never ours; he did, however, have three friends, all called

Tony by bizarre coincidence, none of whom knew each other well but who were all self-made, multi-millionaire entrepreneurs.

To say they fired something in me would be an understatement.

So, shortly after graduating from what one of my old managers called 'Tractor College', I replied to an ad on the back of my parents' daily copy of *The Daily Telegraph*'s appointments pages (when that was a thing) that said: 'Just graduated? Not sure what to do? Call me.'

So I did, and ended up in a pokey little office just off Regent Street (only the second time I'd ever been to London), where this guy asked me a lot of very strange questions about things like tenacity and determination. He seemed to like what I said and so sent me for interviews to Rank Xerox, Alcatel, Canon and Pitney Bowes.

After five interviews, Rank Xerox decided they didn't want me.

The first Alcatel interview was so weird that I declined the second.

Canon offered me a job selling faxes in Leicester, which didn't feel like enough of an adventure despite being the birthplace of my parents.

Pitney Bowes offered me a job in London selling franking machines (mailing meters) – I didn't know what they were, but I did fancy living in London, having been there three times by that point!

Despite some phenomenal training, I turned out to be a distinctly average salesperson who was just about successful enough to secure a job as a sales trainer at Head Office in an Essex town called Harlow (oh, the glamour) a couple of years later.

And I loved it.

For pretty much the first time in my life, I found something I was naturally good at and thoroughly enjoyed.

Unfortunately, the money stank, and I'd lived in London long enough to have acquired some expensive tastes, so when the opportunity arose to get a sales team management role, I leapt at it.

For the second time I found myself in a job I loved and could do.

The team I took over were based in the North West of the UK and were the worst performing out of 27 teams in the country. Two years later we were number one, so I promptly left to crystalise that on my CV – oh, and I'd met an amazing girl, now my wife and mother to our two beautiful daughters, who was living in the south and who I'd decided I wanted to marry if she was foolish enough to have me.

Punching massively above my weight both personally and professionally, I applied for a job, this time on the front page of *The Sunday Times'* appointments pages, no less. This was for a role with AT&T, leading a new sales team for them back in London.

Somehow I got it and loved working for AT&T, but nine months later I was seduced by the exuberance of telecoms in the late 1990s and exchanged the security of one of the world's biggest businesses for pre-IPO shares in a startup telecoms company backed by the Estée Lauder family (don't ask!).

So began a four-and-a-half-year rollercoaster that eventually saw me on the board of a $500m telecoms company at the age of 29, leading several hundred people. Enough thrills and spills in that chapter to be a book on its own – and a debt to an MD called Barry that I'll never be able to repay – that sadly ended with the US parent company going into administration when the dot com bubble burst.

For a brief moment, a few of us explored an MBO but fortunately that didn't work out and, just at that time, I got a call from a headhunter seeking a Sales & Marketing Director for a new division of a little company called Barclays Bank – finally someone my mother had heard of!

A thing called the internet was taking off and Barclays, together with Accenture, had formed BarclaysB2B, a very early venture in an electronic trading platform for businesses.

Over the course of a year, I helped lead this business to some growth but it fairly quickly moved back to its rightful home as part of Accenture and not Barclays.

At that point I was off again to look at the appointments pages but got a most unexpected call from a senior Barclays executive, literally just as I was about to leave. He wanted me to stay on for a further six months and work with their corporate bankers to help improve their sales skills.

No team, no budget, no office, no big fancy title; I thought I'd hate it, but guess what? I loved it!

A spark was fired in me that perhaps if one company was willing to pay me to do a non-job then maybe more might be and perhaps even several at the same time...

My non-job

Whilst those early entrepreneurial seeds were still there, I'd never really done anything about them. I'd been building a career, getting ever-fancier job titles and making more and more of a nuisance of myself attempting (occasionally successfully, often not) to drive change and growth.
The non-job at Barclays changed all of that.

What I'd thought was a six-month tour of being a paid troublemaker turned into the most important moment of my entire professional career – and I'll never be able to thank those who enabled it enough.

Of course my wife saw it coming long before I did.

We'd just had our second daughter and were living through everything that two under two throws at you – and then I turned up with the news that I was going to have to find another job less than a year after a somewhat ignominious exit from the world of telecoms!

How she not only managed to stay calm but also encourage me to consider doing the non-job sort of work as a full-time business, whilst holding down a demanding full-time job of her own, is beyond me to this day.

Sleep deprived and sitting in our garden in the late summer of 2002, we decided that I'd give it a go for a year and if it didn't work, well, never mind, I'd just go back to corporate life.

Now, to be clear, Barclays were very generous given how little time I'd spent with them and that, together with a relatively prudent approach to saving in the previous few years, meant we had a bit of a cushion (a runway as we'll call it later in this book) and I've only come to realise how vital that was over the subsequent years.

So, as the autumn progressed into winter and the final monthly pay cheques came in, my wife and I set up a company!

I spent several happy hours in an office stationery store buying stackable in/out trays, a marvellous stapler, enough Sellotape to wrap the house in and more envelopes than you can imagine.

I actually only recently threw out the boldly coloured in/out trays, having never used them once.

Not sure what I was thinking but, of the things I wasted my time on in those first few months, the visit to the stationery store actually ranks quite low!

The big mistake I made – and how often do we see people make the same mistake – was to believe that if I built it, they would come.

So, following the investment in pencils etc, there came a logo, a website and of course a 'proposition'.

Every book I'd read, indeed every business I had led, believed messianically in the religion of proposition – and for most businesses that's exactly the right thing to believe in.

Just not, as it turns out, in consulting.

But I didn't know that then, so I used my shiny new laptop to develop a series of impressive slides that proclaimed the discovery of a blend of consulting alchemy hitherto unheard of.

I then trotted off to various old colleagues and shared my genius with them.

Because they were all (generally) very nice people who didn't want to rain on my probably slightly over-exuberant parade, they told me I had nailed it.

Back home I went, like a conquering warrior with stories of great triumph.

No invoices to send, you understand, but wow, those stories!

Now at this point I should share an important piece of extra information.

In my final months of my non-job at Barclays, I'd been lucky enough to meet several senior leaders who had all briefly considered giving this non-banker a leadership role in their division of Barclays.

Very briefly as it turns out.

Seems that relevant experience is quite important when leading teams lending millions, and I certainly didn't have any of that.

"

No one has ever bought
what I think I am – they
have bought what they
think I am.

"

What I've always had, though, is an innate curiosity about people and business and so, as a result of a lot of questions – some of them apparently quite good (look for the dynamite this became later in the book), a couple of these leaders said that if I was ever to become a con-sultant (an alternative path I'd been nervously gabbing about) then they would be interested in hiring me to do for them what they'd seen me do in the tiny division I'd been helping to run before.

You see, I was known as a pretty decent sales leader and, to cut a long story short, very soon after I left Barclays I won a couple of very small contracts to deliver some sales training for them.

To be clear, this wasn't my sophisticated genius prop-osition that I'd been peddling but, as what I stupidly saw then as a stop gap, they seemed fine and I was grateful, though only in hindsight do I realise quite how grateful I should have been.

As I'm sure you've worked out by now, not a single person ever bought my proposition.

No one has ever bought what I think I am – they have bought what they think I am.

As soon as I wised up – just about in time to continue to meet the nappy bill – and stopped talking about me and focused entirely on asking people about them and their businesses, as soon as I stopped trying to sell people what I thought they needed and instead went with what they actually wanted, then real opportunities started to flow.

Not in an immediate torrent, you understand.

Initially, just a little dribble but over time, and as my confidence grew in my approach, one client led to another, engagements started to deepen and diversify. I started to attract opportunities to work with different industries, even in different countries, and slowly but surely what had initially been an ill-informed experiment started to look like it could be an actual permanent thing.

Of course Mrs Crabtree was not remotely surprised.

Building Positive Momentum

I must admit that from day one, whenever I talked about Positive Momentum, I used the collective 'we' when in truth, for the first couple of years, it was just me doing everything.

I suspect most of my clients knew this only too well, but they generously indulged my self-consciousness about being a sole trader and never called me on it.

Looking back, this feels a bit silly. However, I always felt that Positive Momentum was much more than a 'lifestyle business' (oh how I hate that term) and that was also the reason that I didn't give it some self-aggrandising eponymous name like Matt Crabtree Associates.

Even in the early days I secretly dreamt of Positive Momentum becoming a 'proper' business but, in truth, I had absolutely no idea how that might happen (there was certainly no business plan, despite the considerable availability of stationery – I even bought a flipchart, though to this day the only people who ever used it were the kids!) and instead just decided to see how much work I could win and deliver on my own and see where that would take me.

Well, through luck, bad pricing and an agricultural work ethic, within two years I had more work than I could deliver on my own. Worse than that, I was doing invoices at the weekend, diary management (badly) at lunchtimes and preparation on my knees on EasyJet flights.

Since we had also decided that I would not be working any school holidays (that's 12 weeks per year in the UK and something I have stuck to – thanks to Mrs. C – every year since I started) you can imagine that the remaining 40 weeks were becoming mightily congested and we began to wonder why I'd walked away from a six-figure corporate salary, despite the apparent 'success' of this endeavour.

Something had to change, and that started with getting an administrative assistant.

Now, even in those days, virtual assistants proliferated and I could easily have gone down that route. However, I was slowly starting to find that I could command a relative premium for my time based on the experience I'd had at a moderately senior level in corporate life.

In my view a virtual assistant just isn't consistent with a premium consultant and that's a principle we've stuck by ever since, building a fantastic team of home-based (we've been working without offices since 2003 – wfh not new to us!) Executive Assistants, as we now call them.

These professionals have proved utterly invaluable in the building of Positive Momentum and are SO much more than diary managers.

Today my colleagues and I rely on them completely for managing our diverse practices, the frequently urgent demands of our clients and to make sure that when we get home we can dedicate our attention properly to our home lives. We simply could not do it without them and to every PM EA, both past and present, I thank you from the bottom of my heart; we would not be the business we are today without every single one of you.

Of course, the other side of scaling the business was to find people who could deliver on the projects that I had run out of capacity for.

Now here there are two problems.

Firstly, clients were choosing me and persuading them that someone else would be doing the job might cause problems. This is despite the fact that the world is brimming with consultants who are infinitely better at it than me. In fact, today I'm lucky enough to call some of them my colleagues.

Secondly, finding people who are willing to work in a pay-as-you-go manner for a proportion of the fee I'm charging – what the industry calls 'associates'.

Again, I was fortunate enough to find a few early PM pioneers who indeed were willing to work like that and who all had both the interpersonal skills and proven experience to ensure that clients would like them.

And it worked.

For a while.

Unfortunately, over time, what became clear was that I'd unwittingly developed exactly the kind of consulting company that I never liked (actually loathed) when I was a buyer of consulting.

When I was a corporate exec I got mightily sick of consultants/trainers/coaches pitching to me (rarely asking that many questions) and then, when they turned up to do the work, the person I'd met was nowhere to be seen.

It was very irritating, but of course that's the conventional thinking on how you scale a consulting business. The senior partners develop the relationships, win the business and then hand it off to juniors who do the work for a fraction of the rate that the client is paying. The game is to keep layering in as many people as you can into a client to maximise the billing hours.

It's a very well-established business model and it's hard for me to say that the multi-billion dollar businesses that pursue this approach are wrong. It's just not what I wanted Positive Momentum to ever be, and yet it was accidentally becoming so. Something had to change and so, just like many small businesses eager for the next stage of growth but determined to stay true to their purpose, we changed course.

All of the pioneer associates went off with new friends and are all first class business professionals to this day.

They are another group I owe a debt of gratitude to. You know who you are, it's been a while, but thank you.

Around the same time a serendipitous event happened that supercharged Positive Momentum and to this day is the single most meaningful event in our growth story.

I was grabbing a cup of tea with one of my most senior clients in a little outdoor cafe in Central London straight after a session I'd been running with his European management team. It had been a lively session to say the least and I figured he'd be wanting to debrief the meeting and talk about next steps.

But no.

Instead, he told me that he wanted to become a consultant. He liked his role, and was very good at it, but having led very large and complex teams all over the world for nearly 25 years, at that point he felt ready for a change. In fact, he had always felt that his temperament was better suited to consulting – and boy how true did that prove to be.

Now, I am a little slow on the uptake sometimes.

I told him what a good idea that was (whilst inwardly lamenting the loss of a lucrative client and the probable gain of a formidable competitor) and how well I thought he'd do at it. He calmly gave me a look that I've grown used to over the years, and now very highly value, and told me that for a generally perceptive person I was sometimes more than a bit dim!

What had I missed?

Fortunately, he quickly put me out of my misery and told me that he wanted to work with me.

Now, no disrespect to our pioneer associates, but this guy was operating at a level not only considerably more senior than any of them had ever worked but also more senior than I had ever operated, too. The idea that he might join was a revelation, but it put in action a series of events that enabled me to make Positive Momentum everything it is today.

He told me that he'd join me, but on two conditions.

Firstly, he needed to make sure that he could continue earning a multi-six-figure income without a moment's blip to get set up and, secondly, that I would show him exactly how I was finding and winning business on a consistent basis.

Let me be clear. This guy started life as an engineer. When he says 'show me exactly' he means exactly, in detail and then subject to significant scrutiny.

What he didn't want any help with was what he would be doing for clients. He'd already understood what you'll recall it took me a while to learn when I started: that people you know will hire you to help them on a fractional basis with what they think you're good at as long as you don't bamboozle them with some BS proposition.

The good news was that this guy knew LOADS of people who knew he was really good and couldn't wait to borrow him. However, the problem was that he didn't want to do loads of transactional, contracting-style work.

He knew what my rates were – in fact, he used to give me a real hard time about them as a client – and he wanted at least the same, but he was wise enough to know that that game might be different.

So began the development of what we call today our Positive Momentum Operating System, or the PMOS for short.

In five years, I'd never written a thing down about how I was finding and winning business. I'm not sure I even knew there was a formula to it. But he did – he just didn't know what it was and told me that the only way he was going to give me 20% of his billings was if I could precisely define it and then coach him on it live and repeatedly.

So, with just about the best carrot you can imagine, that's exactly what I did and to this day Gary Gamp is a self-proclaimed 'good apprentice'. He sets the standard to which all other PM partners (me very much included) aspire towards.

Since Gary joined me in 2008, he's been followed by more than 60 other partners, both in Europe and India, some of whom are still with us, some of whom have gone off to develop other ventures or brilliant new careers elsewhere, and all of whom have left an indelible mark on a business I could not be more proud of.

A PM partnership today is a franchise. We're all independent but none of us consult either for anyone else or under our own steam. Positive Momentum is our trading identity, the power behind our businesses and an exclusive community of like-minded, experienced professionals that a partner can tap into as much or as little as they like.

We've created a near frictionless environment for our partners. No dumb processes, rules, ceremonies or systems. We work to both the letter and spirit of the law but we're allergic to anything else that slows us down, makes us difficult to do business with or gets in the way of time with family and friends.

Positive Momentum isn't just our name, it's our code.

Why I'm writing the book I wish I'd read all those years ago

These days I read a lot of books. But I never did as a kid – hence the educational problems highlighted earlier – but once I found an interest in business there was no stopping me.

Thanks to an amazing Zimbabwean friend I met at agricultural college, the first business book I read at the age of 20 was the story of Lee Iacocca, the first non-Ford family member to run Ford and the saviour of the Chrysler brand in the 1960s – and I was instantly hooked. The politics, the intrigue, the strategy, the highs and the lows – I was utterly fascinated and have been ever since.

It's no surprise that the moment I'd decided I was going to give consulting a try, I was scouring a then nascent little book site called Amazon for anything that might tell me what I should be doing. And I found several books that seemed to be exactly what I was looking for.

The titles suggested that a guaranteed path to success as an independent consultant was available for as little as £14.99, and so – next to my shelf of brand new (but empty to this day) box files – I started to develop a small library of 'how-to' manuals.

These variously advised me to choose a niche, develop a proposition, build an elevator pitch, write a business plan, even write a book – well, better late than never!

Just as Gary later coined, I was a 'good apprentice' but some of this just didn't seem right to me. I'd spent nearly 15 years in corporate life across four different organisations, ending up at a reasonably senior level, and most of my career moves seemed to come about not because of pushy transactional sales skills – we've already established that wasn't my forte, even in the heady days of the early nineties selling franking machines – but much more because I invested in relationships.

Wasn't getting consulting gigs just like getting a new job or a promotion, just again and again with different firms and at the same time? If it was, then I knew I was good at that.

Following my false start with my consulting alchemy proposition – the approach strongly advocated by the how-to books – I set these aside and took what I thought was a highly differentiated approach instead, only to discover much later that what I was doing was exactly the same as the 'hidden-in-plain-sight' approach of the managing partners of the massive global consulting firms.

I'm writing this book 19 years after I first started in this fantastic business, and it is specifically for anyone who wants the freedom, fulfillment and, yes, security of this type of professional existence.

I'm writing this book to save you the years of frustration, wasted effort and misdirection that can so easily be brought about by well-meaning advice from business friends who've never walked this path and how-to books rather too often written by only moderately successful consultants who are deluded enough to think they might make money from a book!

And of course, I'm writing this book to save you a small fortune in stationery costs!

CHAPTER 2

My Approach

The 10 Year Anniversary Lunch

MY FOUNDER CUSTOMERS

This picture was taken in January 2013, 10 years to the month after I left my last full-time job to become an independent consultant.

I took these seven amazing people out for lunch at the chef's table of a restaurant called Pétrus in the fashionable Knightsbridge district of London and it was the most expensive food – and quite a bit more wine than I'd expected to be honest – I'd ever purchased.

And if it had cost 10 times as much, I would still have very gladly paid for it.

You see, these seven people are what I call my founder clients and there is nothing they could ask of me that I wouldn't bend over backwards to do for them.

I can track every client, every partner and every single penny, cent, yen and rupee that I've ever billed back to one of these seven people. Without each of them, I'm certain I would have failed in my consulting endeavours, ended up back in a full-time corporate job and not now be leading the professional and personal life I love so much.

Three of the seven never directly hired me and the remaining four no longer do, but the approach to winning and delivering projects that they unknowingly set in motion has become the foundation of the system both I and my colleagues in Positive Momentum adopt to this day – and every working day.

As amazing and invaluable as these people were (and still are) let me be clear that they were not at the C level of their businesses (except one who was the owner-manager of his own small business) when I started out. Most had no direct decision-making power at that time and were simply good enough to gain me consideration by others who did.

These were the people who saw beyond my deluded early proposition. They knew me – some well, others less so – and had made their own mind up about what they thought I was good at, no matter what propaganda I tried to push at them.

Three of them were former colleagues who'd endured me either as a peer or manager, two of them were other senior leaders elsewhere in Barclays who I was 'lucky' (more later on how to be luckier) enough to meet during my last six months with the bank, one was a former business partner from my telecoms days and one was simply a guy who sat at the back of a speech I gave in my first year, at which I'd suggested that if you don't love your job you should leave – and he resigned the next day!

In fact, this story is probably the best example of the approach that this book lays out for you to follow.

During my first 12 months as an independent consultant, Barclays paid me to give talks to small groups of bankers on how to drive growth (not that I was selling the 'product' of me giving talks at this stage, by the way, it just came up in conversation with someone who thought I'd be good at it).

I'd developed a closing party piece on how it's pretty hard to represent a business you no longer believe in passionately and how if that ever happens you should leave. To my great surprise I got a call the very next day from a guy called Tom (far right in the photo) who I'd never met but who had got my number from someone else and wanted to tell me he'd been in the audience the previous day and had resigned that morning!

Initial horror turned to relief when he told me that he'd been planning this for many months, and was, with a heavy heart, leaving Barclays but had been offered a fantastic promotion with a rival bank.

Since he'd been kind enough to give me a call, we chatted for a while and I asked him a lot of questions about his situation and discovered (amongst many other things) that this career transition had prompted him to take his young family to Disney World in Florida, though he revealed that he wasn't sure about spending the whole time with Mickey!

As luck would have it we'd been there the year before and my wife (our vacation planner extraordinaire in residence) had bought a book called *A Brit's Guide to Orlando* to ensure we'd be just as happy outside of the confines of the Happiest Place on Earth.

After Tom had called, I asked someone for his address and I sent him a copy of that same book.

Small acts of kindness
should need no financial
reward in themselves,
but if you do these kinds
of things deliberately
often enough, I'm living
proof that prosperity in
all respects will flow.

No particular ulterior motive, I just thought he'd like the book.

Of course, as soon as he got the book he called again to say thanks and this time assured me that he'd be introducing me to his new boss at the new bank who he thought I'd really get on with.

Now, if I had a pound...

But, to my genuine surprise, several months later he did indeed get back in touch.

He told me what a great time he and his family had had both within and beyond Disney, how they'd used the book almost every day and how he'd organised for me to meet with his new boss Roy (who became another pivotal contact in my network as well as a great mentor and friend).

This single event led directly to several million pounds of consulting work with Tom's employer that intensified considerably during the aftermath of the financial crisis and has led indirectly to hundreds of other contacts and contracts.

All because I sent a book?

Well, of course not *only* because I sent a book, but I'm certain that none of these events would have happened in this example if I hadn't.

And I've since done this kind of thing hundreds and hundreds of times.

The truth, of course, is that it doesn't lead to contracts anything like every time.

Small acts of kindness like these should need no financial reward in themselves, but if you do these kinds of things deliberately often enough, I'm living proof that prosperity in all respects will flow.

What you need

One of the world's largest and best known management consulting companies call themselves 'The World's Trusted Advisor' and this is the fundamental ethos that sits at the centre of my operating system too.

They continually earn themselves the right to be on the speed dial list of the great and the good in the world and, whilst I can't rival their level of access, I use my version of their principles to build and maintain trusted advisor status relationships. These provide me with a consistent stream of fascinating conversations that often enough lead to commercial opportunities.

My proven and practical (almost agricultural) system will help you to broaden, deepen and maintain your network of contacts who might one day (maybe today, maybe in five years) think of you as a trusted advisor in some respect, without you ever having to come off as a pushy salesperson.

It takes time, patience and persistence but the reward will be a 'practice' that will provide you with freedom, fulfillment and security for many, many years.

It all starts with getting over the idea that you need to work out what your pitch (or worse, your USP ☹) is

45

going to be. So many promising consulting careers are over before they even start due to ill-informed consulting virgins rushing around to their contacts telling them what they think they can do for them.

Most people politely tell you how great that sounds and that they'll be sure to call you the moment they need some of that. And then the phone doesn't ring.

Or at least it doesn't ring often enough for your supply to outstrip the demand from your network and so you never get into the premium rate territory that our system is designed to ensure you achieve.

How close I came to this fate...

Over many years of trial and error I've learnt that success comes down to three key factors, which I'll be practically teaching you throughout this book. They come into play at every stage of the journey, from starting out to winning repeat contracts:

1. Stay visible

It's impossible to overestimate the importance of being in regular contact with your network, but the manner in which you do this really, really matters and we're going to explore that in great detail in this book to ensure you adopt an approach that you and your contacts will want to experience over and over again.

Goldman Sachs (and they do OK, I think?!) believe so strongly in a principle they call Long Term Greedy that they've even written a book about it[1]. It's not actually a great book but the principle is genius, and as soon as I heard one of their MDs talk about it at an event I'd talked my way into on the top floor of their 200 West Street, NYC HQ a few years ago, I realised that this was exactly what I'd been doing all along. In simple terms, it means investing in individual relationships for the long term and not obsessing about when or even whether a commercial opportunity might arise. For Goldmans that might be about an IPO, M&A transaction or other financing event at some indeterminate point in the future. For a simple independent consultant like me, it's about the right confluence of events that might trigger a need for whatever the contact thinks I'm good at.

Success therefore is about being connected and easily accessible to a wide community of contacts at just the right moment for them.

As my story illustrates, your founder customers don't need to be captains of industry. They just need to be people who think you're great at something and have some degree of access and influence.

But let's be clear here, scale does matter.

To find my seven founder clients (my 'princesses and princes', if you will) I met face to face with more than a

---

1 *Long Term Greedy: The Triumph of Goldman Sachs* by Nils Lindskoog

47

hundred individual contacts in the first six months and, though I suspect my frog-kissing technique at that time could have been a lot better, that volume of effort hasn't really changed to this day.

As an inelegant proxy for the scale of your current network, take a look at your total current LinkedIn connections.

Divide that number by the number of years you've been in business post-education.

Between 100 and 200 and you're in good shape.

More than 250 and you might be over-connected.

Less than 50 and, whilst it's certainly not a showstopper, we've got a lot of work to do.

Now, if you're phobic about social media generally (or LinkedIn in particular) please don't freak out and throw this book against the wall!

I'm not about to tell you that you need to start posting pictures of cats to get attention. Your digital presence certainly matters but those who tell you it's the path to consulting riches more or less on its own are charlatans and should be ignored.

I have so much more to say on elegantly maxing your visibility later but, suffice to say at this point, if you're hoping for some cheesy email newsletter template, LinkedIn banner ad design or an SEO strategy that will magically create leads from potential clients who neither know you nor anyone you know, you're going to be very, very disappointed...

2. Play chess

In a game of chess, after both players make their first move, 400 possible board setups exist. After the second pair of turns, there are 197,742 possible games, and after three moves, 121 million.

Turning a contact into a consulting contract is much like this. It's not a repeatable cookie-cutter process, and anyone who tells you it is has probably never won many consulting contracts

This is not sudoku.

It's chess, and I'm going to show you how to become a grand master of the consulting chess game. So many rookie consultants make their first bad move in meetings with potential clients by making it all about themselves and by being practically rabid for a contract.

The pros know that the key is to get the other person talking first – and a lot.

That starts by having prepared something more interesting and insightful to ask than bland, boring questions like 'how's business?' That's the commercial equivalent of 'do you come here often?' in my view.

Of course many people you meet either feign or even have real interest in you and can so easily prompt you into talking too much about yourself. At the risk of mixing my game play metaphors, this is when your tennis skills need to come to the fore. Answer politely but get the ball back on their side of the court as soon as you can with another brilliantly constructed question.

The better you become at this art, the more likely it is that your potential client will reveal something that might ultimately lead to an engagement for your superpower(s).

Let's be clear, we're not trying to manipulate anyone here. Organisations always have problems that they can't fix themselves. That's not because they are bad but because running an organisation of practically any size is really, really difficult.

These conversations are designed to gently, respectfully reveal where these difficulties lie and to perhaps, just maybe, start the process of them linking your perceived competencies to the treatment of their ailments.

In essence, it's about being exceptionally curious 100% of the time.

It's not about you.

It's about them, and you developing the certainty that there is always more to know about your contacts and their organisations. The more you attune your antenna, the better you'll equip yourself to spot the moments to nudge your network with a well-timed contact and seed that luck that I've enjoyed for so long.

As we're going to explore in much more detail, one of the most valuable things we can do for clients is to ask them really good questions that give them the space to come up with their own conclusions – and with truly great consultants that starts long before a commercial engagement is agreed.

The best consultants sell clients what they want and earn the right to sell them what they need.

You might want to read that sentence again.

Coming to consulting in the second half of your career is mostly a blessing, but it is also ever so slightly a curse. You'll have seen a lot and, as a result, it will be very tempting to show potential clients how very clever you are by presenting your prescription somewhat prematurely, before the potential patient has revealed all of their symptoms.

Now you might get lucky and they might bite, but much more likely they'll immediately feel you're trying to sell to them and either row back from the severity of their previously claimed symptoms or simply just clam up.

Worse than that, the next time you get in touch for a 'catch-up' they'll remember your antics and will find various busy excuses to gently rebuff your meeting invitation. Play it right, however, and, like a busy day in Washington Square Park, you'll set up multiple games of chess offering you the diverse pipeline of short, medium and long-term opportunities so essential to a feast and famine-less, sustainable practice.

3. Deliver distinctively

Consultants and consulting companies don't always enjoy fabulous reputations. The old 'reading your watch to tell you the time' stereotype is alive and well and sadly many consultants offer little more to their clients.

(In fact, a belief that there had to be a better way was a big part of the catalyst for me setting up a consulting business. In my early days, I even arrogantly characterised myself as 'the antidote to consulting' but soon realised that was a petard too easy to be hoisted by and that anyway there's actually a lot of very good consulting companies in the world.)

The seeds of this malaise are normally set by projects with flaky expected outcomes.

If you don't know what your client is trying to achieve at the highest level – and aren't constantly monitoring this, as clients do love a new strategy every few years/months/minutes – and you haven't linked your endeavours to that, then please don't be surprised by a spreadsheet jockey who you've never met suddenly popping up with some annoying questions you won't be able to answer and a subsequent drastic decline in billing revenues.

Worse than too little proven value, some consultants can be a royal pain in the backside to employees of the client, abusing their executive relationships (which they often confuse with air cover) and treating everyone else with patronising disdain.

Understanding and working effectively within the political environment – at every level of your client – is vital to long-term success since today's receptionist might very well be tomorrow's senior manager and, in any event, any senior manager worth their salt will be watching closely to see how well you treat more junior members of their team.

This also includes how professional and respectful you remain with the odd client-side antagoniser.

I'll admit that I used to mess with consultants a bit when I was client side, just to see how they'd react! Not necessarily my proudest moments but subsequent experience/payback suggests I was far from alone.

Of course, the most irritating habit of all is consulting companies who layer in more and more (often very junior) team members as they wheedle out more and more supposed problems they can fix. This rarely ends well and is a classic symptom of firms with big fixed costs and short-termist thinking.

I often ask newer Positive Momentum consultants whether they would prefer to make $20k per year, every year for 10 years from a client or $100k in the next 12 months from that same client and nothing ever again.

Of course, this is a silly hypothetical but I do enjoy (probably a bit too much) watching the cogs of intelligent people get a bit mashed by this.

None of this is to say you should shy away from further opportunities with existing clients. Just that you should always be able to justify further engagements as a result of the measurable value you've added so far. We call it 'the CFO test' and I'm going to give you lots more on how to pass this with flying colours later on.

Why it works

I became an independent consultant because I wanted to spend 100% of my time doing the stuff I do best.

The truth is that I was hard work as an employee.

As a former boss once told me, *'You're not very good at playing "Emperor's new clothes", in fact you've a distinct habit of regularly pointing, with some enthusiasm, at our nakedness!'*

When I told my last boss that I was thinking of leaving to become a consultant he said, *'I think it's probably best.'* That stung a bit until he followed it up with, *'We love having you around, just in small doses!'*

Despite what some might describe as early career success, I got the message and found an existence where being like this is practically what you get paid for, though as I later discovered, with a great deal more finesse than I'd practised as an employee.

But I'm no natural entrepreneur: I'm risk averse and I worry about making the next mortgage payment as much as most people do. I left corporate life with a very young family and enough money to last us about a year, so I had to make this work in relatively short order. Worse than that, I didn't know anyone who had made this transition.

As we've already established, existing books weren't much help. But what I lacked in expertise I more than made up for in work ethic. As I discovered on the farm in the 1980s, cows don't milk themselves, and so I made it my mission to get out and meet with as many people as I could as fast as I could.

As I've shared, pushing a proposition didn't work. I certainly 'failed fast' at that and have since watched countless others fall to the same fate.

Perhaps this approach seems odd, counterintuitive and maybe even contrary to the laws of business you might have previously learnt, but I promise you it works. I've operated this way for nearly 20 years at time of writing, have helped countless others to transform their approach and turn frustration into freedom – and I'm going to do the same for you.

Whilst I can't deny the leap of faith, enormous bow wave of initial effort and then patience that you'll likely need, the reward on the other side will be a network of wonderful contacts (and very likely some fascinating new friends) who have you on speed dial and who seem to hire you with very little effort on your part and rarer and rarer dispute about your price.

No Nonsense Business Expertise is more than my organisation's brand byline. It's what we deliver to our clients and partners and it's what this book is going to give you.

Who it works for

Too many people who would be fabulous consultants never even get started. They tragically talk themselves out of it with weird, unsubstantiated insecurities. Not the right experience, not the right industry, not the right/enough contacts, too old, too young, wrong phase of the moon; I've heard just about all of them.

Of course, it's far from the right choice for everyone – and in the next chapter we'll explore if it's right for you in much more detail – but assuming you've been in business for more than a decade, have found something you're really good at (not the best ever, just really good is enough) and are a likeable human being who hasn't irritated too many people in your career so far, then you've everything you need to succeed as an independent consultant.

You don't need to have been a particularly big cheese – or even know that many grand fromages! However, as I'm sure you've worked out by now, you do need to be the kind of person who is prepared to play the long game. If you're an instant gratification sort of person, then our system (indeed, I'd suggest consulting generally) isn't for you.

Whether you're just wondering about making the move out of a full-time role and into independent consulting, or you are already doing it but just not as successfully as you would like, then this book is for you.

Whether your career so far has been in selling, buying, building, supporting, hiring, or indeed any other function no matter how specialist, then this book is for you.

Whether you see yourself as a consultant, a coach, a trainer, an advisor or have an impressively coloured belt in operational jiu-jitsu (or if your last accreditation was your cycling proficiency test), then this book is for you.

SUMMARY

I've discovered that it's never the shiny proposition that wins in consulting.

It's not the stunning website or even the (probably not) best-selling book.

It's hundreds of little things, some as simple as sending a book to someone that helps them have an amazing holiday with their kids, that in combination and routinely applied make the difference between moderate and massive success, and I'm going to lay out the whole system for you in this book so that you can copy – and no doubt improve upon – it.

Part 2

Moving Out of Corporate

CHAPTER 3

Is Consultancy Right For You?

The Power of Your Why

One of our most consistently successful consulting partners ever was an HR Director in the UK division of a famous FMCG company when I first met her.

She was very good at her job, immensely well-liked by her colleagues (despite sometimes being the bearer of bad news) and had previous experience in a number of other well-known firms across the finance, legal and consulting sectors. There is no doubt that her stellar corporate career could have continued unabated, but she'd arrived at a crossroads in her life.

At the time, her two young sons were just starting at school and she wanted to find a way to be the best parent to her lovely boys that she could possibly be, whilst also being fulfilled and productive commercially.

We call this 'your why' and this particular partner had that in abundance.

Funnily enough, however, she also had a 'dream job' in mind, and incredibly that exact job came up – and of course she was targeted – just a year or so after she had started operating as an independent consultant with us.

My first thought was, 'Oh well, it was nice while it lasted but I guess she'll be taking that role' (and maybe she'll hire us when she's got her feet under the table), but no.

Of course she went for interviews and talked at some length with the company. The package was great, the location perfect and the opportunity to make an impact was significant. The fit seemed perfect, the company really wanted her but... she didn't take it.

Why?

Because she'd had a taste of the freedom, fulfillment and flexibility that consulting can offer.

Because she'd found that she was very good at, and rather enjoyed, both delivering projects and attracting new ones.

And most important of all, because she was never missing sports day, parents' evening or any of those thousands of special, never-to-be-repeated moments in her boys' lives.

She found her 'why' and even her dream job wasn't enough to let that go.

This is just one story among thousands. Everyone has a different context, a different reason for considering independent consulting. The key is to find a big enough 'why' and then use it to power your success.

MYTHBUSTERS

The world of independent consulting is full of penniless geniuses. People who can do amazing things in their field but are clueless when it comes to attracting opportunities. They're the ones who are often raging about how no one listens to them and if only their (usually potential) clients would do x or y then things would be better.

They're generally right.

And they're about as suited to being an independent consultant as I am to being a fashion designer.

Unique commercial expertise is rarer than hen's teeth so if you're living in some La-La Land where you believe that there is a long list of people with big problems just desperate for someone like you to make themselves available, then this world really isn't for you.

MINDSET

One day, in a brief moment of respite in the midst of the financial crisis, a client (who themselves were rather at the epicentre of that particular storm) said to me: 'We love working with you, Matt, because you just make everything seem less bad!'

Given the look on the client's face immediately after they had said this, this didn't seem to sound as positive out loud as it had in their head and so they then started to qualify it in that rather British way.

'No, no,' I said, 'I love it! I wish I had the nerve to put it on my business cards.'

In hindsight, what's most striking about this interaction is that the client said *seem* less bad.

Not that I'd actually *made* anything better but simply made it all *seem* less unpleasant.

I'm hopeful that I actually had more impact than that – indeed, having vocalised her view, she tried to persuade me that I had – but in that moment for that client what I was doing represented value and that was good enough.

Consultants exist to make an organisation (be it a single person, a team, a process, a proposition or whatever they are working on) better.

Not perfect, just better than it was before they were hired.

It's a tough lesson, and perhaps you'll even feel it lacks a degree of substance, but if you're on some crusade to completely solve some widespread, long-standing business ailment then you're either an extremely rare genius, have significant personal wealth or (more likely) you're sadly deluded.

At the very least, you're facing an uphill battle to convince potentially fee-paying clients that you've discovered the elixir to their hitherto irresolvable issues.

In the nearly 100 years since the likes of Alfred P. Sloan (author of the legendary book and one of many required reads as a consultant, *My Years With General Motors*) roamed the boardrooms of organisations, the world of business has become both significantly more efficient and infinitely more complex.

Modern leaders have a dizzying array of priorities that can often seem to be in contradiction with each other. How to meet the seemingly insatiable growth appetite of shareholders *and* tread much more lightly on the planet? How to automate processes *and* keep employees feeling valued? How to ferment a spirit of constant innovation whilst at the same time keep delivering on existing commitments?

Running an organisation is hard and it's only getting harder.

Enter the experienced, empathetic and above all pragmatic independent consultant. The second chapter professional who knows exactly how tough it is to thrive in the middle of this mêlée and who, now they are free of the structure of a full-time role, can see the wood for the trees just a little better.

The value of this experience and approach is immense but as Spider-Man (sorry!) famously said, 'With great power comes great responsibility.'

Operating as a third party to help an organisation to improve takes both subject matter expertise *and* world class diplomacy.

In fact, the same conundrum exists in people seeking internal job promotion into a role where there is a problem. Do I tell my potential new boss why I'm the right person to fix the somewhat dysfunctional team they themselves have overseen or do I suck up and tell them what a brilliant function they've built and how I'd love to be a part of it?

It's the age-old 'no one wants to be told their baby is ugly' story and a lack of understanding of the importance of walking this tightrope effectively has been the death of many a potentially glittering consulting career.

Believing that once you're no longer on the payroll you're somehow exempt from the previously applicable, unwritten rules of internal politics is yet another dangerous delusion.

Any idiot can waltz into an organisation and, to coin my last boss's phrase, 'tell everyone that the emperor is in fact naked'.

Pointing out what's not working is easy. Coming up with workable ideas that make things better in the specific client's context and delivering them in a way that does not bite the hand that might be willing to feed you, now that's the real art (and value) of consulting.

Of course, all of this presupposes that you've made peace with stepping off the career ladder and losing all that comes with that.

Whilst you might ultimately enjoy significant soft power, as a consultant you'll never again have sign-off or any kind of formal influence.

We intentionally, indeed necessarily, exist behind the scenes.

Our role is only to make others look good (or at least better).

Our advice is routinely ignored.

Our successes will rarely be acknowledged, though our failures will enjoy significant publicity.

It's a high stakes game with no chance of a salary increase or stock options when it all goes brilliantly. The best you can hope for is quiet appreciation, a promptly paid invoice and perhaps the opportunity to help again when another issue arises that matches your particular skills, as the client perceives them.

The reading and research to stay relevant is relentless, as is the need to keep visible to potential new clients whilst simultaneously delivering diligently to those you've already won.

Not to mention the frequent proposals you'll sweat to construct only to receive radio silence for weeks and then to discover that the client has decided that the problem you'd brilliantly synthesised is not actually such an issue after all.

Of course, the constant tyre kicking from people who are suspicious, even cynical, of consultants (just like I was) is a never-ending joy too.

If all that doesn't sound particularly enticing, then I'm achieving my aim here.

Too many people have punctuated (and in some cases terminally damaged) their careers with sojourns into a world that they discovered was not as they had imagined. Independent consulting is not for everyone and if this book helps just one person to avoid the frustration and pain that entering into this on false pretences can create then I'll be very happy.

On the other hand, the freedom, fulfillment and security that independent consulting offers are really something else.

1. Freedom

For nearly 20 years – and since day one, long before I could really afford it – I've taken all the school holidays as vacation; in the UK that's 12 weeks per year.

I vividly remember my eldest daughter – then just 7 – returning home from a midweek play date during the Easter school holidays and asking me why her friend's daddy wasn't at home at lunchtime. Until then she believed that all parents didn't go to work when their kids were off school.

I loved that she thought it was normal – but I was sad to explain to her the reality for most people.

Arguably, I bailed out of a conventional career construct early and was perhaps well on the way to even bigger roles (or possibly to a massive Peter principle comeuppance) but there isn't a single unrealised promotion, bonus or stock option that could have compensated for the long and frequent holidays I've been able to enjoy with my family.

Once you've taken your first three week holiday, anything shorter will have you feeling shortchanged.

(NOTE – none of this is to say that I've never taken a call, sent an email or even worked with the occasional client during the school holidays; in fact, we've been to some amazing places in the world as a family off the back of client engagements. It's simply that for very nearly two decades, at time of writing, no boss has ever told me I need to be somewhere at a time that's not agreeable to my family.)

Talking of bosses, the freedom to be your own is something to cherish too. I've been lucky and had some amazing bosses in my career, but I'm acutely aware that not everyone is so fortunate.

The reality that we all know is that not everyone is suited to leadership but somehow getting under the people leadership radar isn't as hard as it should be and so who your boss is becomes a kind of lottery. Draw the wrong numbers and working life becomes much harder than it should be, rather too often infecting every other part of your life too.

Of course, you also lose the chance to find that great boss who sees things in you that you'd previously not seen in yourself. That's why a network of mentors and even paid coaches is vital to your success and we'll talk much more about that later.

Consulting also represents freedom from some of the more humdrum elements of organisational life.

Whilst running your own business is far from free of bureaucracy (thanks national tax authorities but hello experts you can outsource to), the fact that you never have to attend a monthly meeting where Bob from Accounts or Sally from IT drones on about overrunning and over-budget Project Zeus, telling us all things we either knew already or just don't believe. Well, let's just say these are not ceremonies I hugely miss...

2. Fulfillment

Like most people, there were parts of my jobs that I was great at and parts that I just wasn't suited to.

I loved coaching but wasn't great at the annual appraisal round (happily a dying concept).

I wasn't bad at putting together and delivering pre-sentations, but monthly reports never really rocked my world – sorry former bosses for all the late submissions.

Motivating teams to deliver was right up my street but keeping the Gantt chart up to date... well, you get the idea. As I've said already, I'm aware that I wasn't always a great employee.

Discovering independent consulting has been the greatest professional gift of my career. It has meant that I've been able to stay fully engaged with business life – which I love, in case that's not totally obvious yet – but only the bits that I'm good at.

Every day offers a fascinating new challenge and the fact that I get handsomely paid for dispensing my opinion still feels like a bonus, though please don't tell any of my clients that!

Over the years, I've met many people who've fallen out of love with corporate life and think that consulting is a good alternative route.

I'll tell you what I've told all of them.

Go open a beach bar.

To be a success as a consultant you've got to embrace all of the flaws, imperfections and dysfunctions of organi-sational life. Not only is it because of them that consulting is even a thing, but the joy of helping organisations to improve and people to thrive in spite of them has to be something that consistently sparks your passion.

If that's not you, then mine's a piña colada.

One of the greatest myths told about independent consulting is that it's somehow less secure than a full-time role.

3. Security

One of the greatest myths told about independent consulting is that it's somehow less secure than a full-time role.

At time of writing, I've 18 separate billing engagements.

Every client is just as important as the other but I'm not dependent on a single one of them to make the rent. If you have a 'proper job' that's just not the case for you.

I don't want to alarm you but, as you may already have experienced, at any moment your livelihood could be in peril for reasons that are completely beyond your control.

For example, in the year 2000 I had my dream job with an amazing team working for a great boss in a booming industry. Then all of a sudden our parent company in the US went into something called Chapter 11 as a result of not being able to raise more funds from a place called Nasdaq whose typical investors had suddenly (and en masse) decided that funding a global telecoms company wasn't as interesting as they'd said it was the day before.

It all happened 5,000 miles away from where I was working and it had not a single thing to do with how well (or not) I was doing my job. A very nice man from a company called PWC came to my office (oh yes, I had one of those!) and told me that despite what I'd previously considered to be my very great importance to our mission, my services were no longer required and I'd need to join a (very long as it turned out) queue for anything that was owed to me.

Variations on this story are sadly not rare. From reorganisations to mergers and bad bosses to discrimination, the myriad uncontrollable ways your role can be threatened would keep you awake at night if you focused on them too much.

Of course, in the light of this reality the sensible thing to do is to keep your resume polished, your LinkedIn profile and activity in tip-top shape and even go for the odd role with an alternative employer irrespective of how happy you are in your current role.

My eldest brother (who worked in a big industry but with very few players) always used to go for interviews with competitors when they approached him. His bosses were always aware – because he used to tell them what he was doing.

He retired a few years ago after more than 25 years with the same company.

He never left.

But constantly looking for something better kept them on their toes. As he taught me: looking isn't leaving.

But what if you've tried this approach and still haven't found that dream job? Perhaps companies would just be happier borrowing instead of buying you? Since I set up as an independent consultant on 1 January 2003, I've had not a single approach about a full-time role.

No headhunter calls.

No clients loving my work so much they want to hire me.

Nada.

Now, to be honest, in the early days I wondered what the hell had happened. At that point the consulting thing was in truth a bit of an experiment and a big part of me suspected that before too long someone would waft a big sexy job under my nose and that I'd be powerless to resist the allure of the salary/title/office/equity/car; all these things that I used to consider important.

It had all been so easy before and I genuinely couldn't understand why all of a sudden it had stopped. I'm now eternally grateful that it did.

On a whiteboard wall in my home office I've a series of concentric circles with my original five clients in the centre. (You remember my expensive lunch friends from the last chapter?)

Each subsequent circle shows the connection between one client and the next.

Every connection tells a story.

People leave one organisation and take me with them to their next.

People from one organisation recommend my services to someone in another organisation.

Even suppliers to one client hearing of me and start hiring me for themselves.

All seemingly serendipitous but in fact consciously but subtly propagated.

Whilst to this day I'm still working with many clients from the inner circles, I'm up to seven layers beyond those five original core clients. As my Positive Momentum colleagues will wearily attest, I'm obsessed with this ever-evolving whiteboard creation. It's proof that this system works and that once you've got it running well (and I admit that can take some years) then you'll enjoy substantially more security than you can ever possibly get in a full-time role.

And finally, are you over the career thing, at least for now?

As we've already explored, you need to have made peace with stepping off the career ladder, but that doesn't mean you can't step back onto it again at some point. In fact, some consultants who've joined Positive Momentum have even initially run twin-track strategies where they've quietly pursued full-time roles whilst seeing if this independent consulting lark might really be for them. Nothing inherently wrong with that, especially if the cash burn rate at home is significant.

However, you've got to take care that your network doesn't get confused about who you are now or worse, begin to think you're only doing consulting as a stop gap. Early conversations that include the sympathetic 'Ah, don't worry, a proper job will come around soon' statements are common when starting up as an independent consultant and you need a robust response to that if you want to be taken seriously. I've post-rationalised that everyone's sudden allergy to offering me roles was because I gave off the aura that I was serious about this from day one. True or not, I've since helped hundreds of people to put a confident foot forward without completely killing any rare golden geese who might just want to lay a golden egg job.

The bigger question is whether you feel genuinely satisfied with the level you attained in your corporate career. If you're still hankering after that bigger job, then perhaps what you need is a really good career coach rather than a complete change of direction. All of my most consistently successful colleagues could easily get another job if they really wanted one. They each stepped out of their careers long before they'd reached their full potential, indeed several of them had (indeed, still have) CEO-level potential. They each know that but they each (I hope) have not a single regret. Whilst they could have become more senior in the conventional way of thinking, it just wasn't what they wanted any more. Instead, they wanted a way to stay active and engaged commercially but without the noise (and indeed lack of security) that can surround a conventional career.

TOOLKIT

So, let's bring all this down to a checklist to help determine whether or not this is a step you can reasonably safely make.

1. Do you have enough real world experience?

You don't need to have been a board member of a Fortune500 company, but the system I've built is specifically designed to help you secure premium rates from day one and this will depend (at least initially) on your previous roles. Anything less than 10 years in business and an absence of scale leadership experience will likely put you in the commodity/contracting rather than premium/consulting pricing space. What does this mean in real money? Well, in GBP terms and at time of writing it's the difference between £500 – £1500 per day and £2000 – £4000 per day. Whilst £1k per day might sound great in principle, you'll soon find you'll be regularly compared to a very big pool of alternatives (yawn), won't be taking many school holidays off and probably won't have enough time for developing new, interesting and potentially more lucrative lines of enquiry.

TRAP TO AVOID

If you can't make this work on 160 days, it's probably not right for you

At Positive Momentum, we talk in terms of 'yield management'. Just like an airline or a hotel, that starts by determining your inventory. For me, that's 160 days: 40 weeks x 4 days billing per week. I've met lots of independent consultants who talk of 200, even 240 days inventory. They're normally exhausted, irritable and not having a whole heap of fun. If you can't make this work with 160 days of inventory (and you likely won't without the right former experience) then I'd say you're better off keeping the salary plus benefits, irrespective of how crazy your current boss is.

To determine your yield, you need at least a year of trading behind you so that you can take 12 months' worth of billings and divide it by your number of days of inventory. £2k+ and rising and this approach is working for you economically, anything less and perhaps a return to a full-time role is the right course of action.

Those of a more financial disposition will already have calculated that this won't make you a millionaire.

With the right inputs this system will get you a very healthy and reliable multiple six-figure GBP (or currency equivalent) income annually. For a seven-figure income you're going to need something more than I have to offer here; however, becoming an independent consultant using my approach will supercharge your network, which in itself will increase the probability of uber-wealth opportunities if that's your goal.

2. Do you have a skill set you're well known for?

We're not seeking anything extra special here, but you obviously need to have been pretty darn good at the thing you're currently/used to be paid a salary to do. I've seen no end of middle-aged people go off at a tangent and study for a professional qualification (often coaching) and then present themselves to their network with this shiny new skill only to find that their former colleagues never regarded them much for that thing despite what their impressive certificate from the Intergalactic Confederation of Business Coaches says. By all means go and get some extra education but please don't delude yourself that your network is patiently waiting for the new improved you. The old you is almost certainly what they value and if what the old you did doesn't do it for you anymore, please refer to my earlier advice on shore-based drinking establishments.

This isn't to say that you need to stay in your swim lane forever. I started out doing sales stuff with banks and telecoms companies because that's what I was known for and that's where I'd come from. Today, I do leadership, strategy, culture and change stuff (as well as still doing plenty of sales stuff too) with clients in an incredibly diverse range of industries right around the world. If I can do that then you can too, and almost certainly much more quickly than I did since you now hold in your hands the way I did it, whereas I was making it up as I went along and wasting time on daft endeavours.

3. Do you have a strongly held opinion or two?

Whilst knowing how and when to convey your views is crucial (much more on this later) you do need to have a distinctive point of view on what it takes to excel in your area of expertise.

Personally, I don't believe that B2B salespeople ever know their customers well enough, nor do I think that people leaders ever know their direct reports well enough. Hardly astonishing insights but in part these points of view have been enough to catalyse thousands of conversations into many hundreds of invoices.

What are the classic mistakes you see organisations making over and over again? Experience has proven time and again that helping organisations with the basics is at least as valuable as helping them with complex challenges like transitioning to new technologies.

4. Do you have a long enough runway?

In case it's not quite obvious yet, this isn't a get-rich-quick scheme. Building a sustainable network of people with proper money to spend and who see you as a trusted advisor in some respect takes time and you can't be panicking about income in those early months. I've often said that potential clients are like children and animals: they smell fear. One whiff of your rabid need to send them an invoice and the willingness to reveal the issues they are facing, and you might be able to help make less bad, evaporates. In fact, you're going to need to get very good at giving off an air of really not needing their money at all. As I've only discovered very much later, the less you appear to need the work (to a point) the more in demand you become.

So, how much do you need for your runway? Well, we normally work on the principle of having enough cash in reserve that it wouldn't matter if you didn't earn a thing for 12 months. Now that's not based on getting to empty by the twelfth month, nor on living on beans and never going out for a year. You need enough to be able to continue to live a completely normal life (whatever that is for you) for the whole of your first 12 months.

Of Positive Momentum consultants both past and present, I can easily count on one hand the number who've actually ended up billing nothing in the first year but, full disclosure, it has happened. I'm relieved to report that these very few individuals all now enjoy success elsewhere and I'm hopeful that their, albeit difficult and short-lived, experience as an independent consultant has served them in some way in their current endeavours. As I said before, this isn't for everyone.

Happily, I'd need many more hands than I'm equipped with to count those who've got their meter running well before their first anniversary and some who as a result of very good pre-planning (see the next chapter) have smashed every financial expectation they had for this and, as a result, have never looked back. Gary built a whole new beautiful house on the back of his very first year's billings!

The reality is that by the time you get to around your sixth month you're going to have a very good idea of whether this can ultimately work for you or not. If by then, using every tactic this system suggests, you've sent not a single proposal then I'm sorry but the world probably doesn't see you this way and your For Rent sign should probably be changed back to For Sale. However, if you've won even just one engagement in that time (which might feel like beginner's luck) then you're off and running and can look forward to one becoming two, two becoming four and so on until your inventory is soon all sold out.

5. Do you have strong support for at least trying this at home?

It's impossible to overestimate the importance of support at home for this significant change in professional identity. Whether you're the main breadwinner in a large hungry family or live alone and just need to feed yourself, having

CHAPTER 3

the enthusiastic support of your loved ones is fundamental. Nothing is more likely to ferment a noticeable aura of anxiety than the sense that someone you care for deeply is uncertain about you taking this next step.

Now, you might find this is easy and that your other half, if you have one, completely gets it and has been wondering for a while why you've been slogging your guts out for an organisation which in their view grossly under-appreciates you and takes you away from them far too often.

More likely, however, you'll get a mild to extreme look of horror when you first float the idea of forgoing a regular pay cheque, a nice pension and an annual bonus. Partners, parents and friends might just think you've taken leave of your senses and will be found hiding, burning or burying this (and any other demonic) book to help you back to career sobriety.

If that turns out to be the case for you then patience and understanding must be your watchwords (kind of helpful to build these muscles anyway as you'll need them in abundance if you do move forward). Gently show your loved ones how you've really thought this through, why you believe it can work for you, perhaps even introduce them to some people who've walked the same path, if you know any. Give them space (probably weeks, maybe months) to process the idea. Answer their (potentially numerous and repetitive) questions about the whys and

84

wherefores of this. Talk them through your career contingency plan, in the event that this didn't actually work out.

But above all else – and specifically for those in a long-term and committed relationship – **don't do this** if you can't get your partner genuinely over the line. We all make compromises for the ones we love and this kind of career change and perceived insecurity (however misunderstood that might be) is just too much of an ask for some partners. Finding your significant other was the gift of your life. Don't create a big issue with them just because you don't like your job as much as you used to. It's not worth it and, in any event, there are going to be days when some of their doubts come true and who needs that thrown back in their face over dinner?!

Now is your time to reflect and think over whether this is the best option for you. Spending this time now will save you time (and worry) later. Please visit the Positive Momentum Network at **www.positivemomentum.com/ network** for links to our self reflection process.

6. Do you like meeting new people (and do you think they like meeting you)?

You don't need to be a life-and-soul-of-the-party type person to succeed as an independent consultant, but equally if you're a I'd-really-rather-not-go-to-the-party type person then this almost certainly isn't for you.

Assuming you're in the 100–200 LinkedIn connections per year of career referenced in Chapter 2, you're already connected to enough people to probably make this work for you, BUT many of these people are simply what we call 'gateway contacts' to others who you don't yet know. They are the amazing people who will get you access but you're going to need to do the heavy lifting of quickly making people like you once that introduction has been made.

And be under no illusion, being likeable is critical to your success.

I've seen consultants who are truly brilliant in their field of expertise but who are unfortunately not very good at making themselves likeable fail horribly, whereas I've also known quite a few who, in truth, have fairly average skill sets but are gracious and engaging with everyone they meet and as a result they succeed. It might not be fair, just or how you'd like the world to be, but it is how the world is...

So, how can you become even more likeable, even if you already feel at the top of your magnetic-personality game?

Just remember the three Es (we consider these so important that they are our company values):

a. Energy

Human beings have an incredible ability to affect the energy levels of each other. We all know people who lazily bang on about their latest ailment, the terrible weather, the morons in government etc, etc. Now don't get me wrong, I get that some people (indeed everyone at one time or another) have some pretty awful stuff to deal with and that being happy clappy 100% of the time is hippy dippy nonsense. Still, if you want to be liked by the broadest community of people (and I hope by now you see the importance of being so) then being a vocal enthusiast for life as much as you possibly can be is a critical tool.

Being energised and optimistic more often than not takes effort, but it is pretty addictive when you see the results.

Some people put this stuff down to personality or genetics but I'm sorry I just think that's self-defeating hogwash and, until someone comes up with a scientifically proven assessment of personality (somebody please save us from the deluge of pseudo-scientific psychometric tests) that states unequivocally 'we are what we are' (argh), I won't be moved on this. As many of the greatest thinkers of the last century, from Dale Carnegie in the 1930s to Simon Sinek in the 2020s, have extolled in ways much more erudite than this: your attitude is a choice. And a choice made repeatedly becomes a habit.

I'm not personally descended from a long line of positive people; indeed in some cases quite the opposite! I wasn't always able to convey a (mostly) sunny disposition until I was taught in my early 20s how to do so and why it matters. It took (and still takes) daily effort and commitment. I still have to contend with a minority of people who, for reasons that remain a mystery to me, want to break down my version of the world. I've learnt to treat

87

those who feel this way with empathy, respect and tolerance, but I've also learnt how to make sure they can't infect me no matter what they say.

What does this mean to the day-to-day life of an independent consultant?

▶ Pay people frequent compliments, both face-to-face and online.

▶ Tell stories of others' triumph and success rather than doom and disaster.

▶ Become allergic to and never initiate judgmental conversations about the failings of others.

▶ Read inspiring books (start with the brilliant *Factfulness: Ten Reasons We're Wrong About the World - and Why Things Are Better Than You Think* by Hans Rosling) and watch uplifting, life-affirming movies at least as much as the daily social media/mainstream news neg-fest.

▶ Stay as fit as you are able.

▶ Smile and laugh often.

b. Engagement

In later chapters, we're going to dive deeply into the why and how of becoming phenomenally engaging, but as a very small amuse-bouche to the upcoming entrée, consider whether you're the kind of person who is routinely and intelligently inquisitive, tends to ask lots of questions of others and is told you're a great listener, or whether you're more of a transmitter preferring the beguiling sound of your own voice to the noise of others.

This key skill didn't (and still doesn't) come naturally to me but like staying fit, I work at it every day, keep it at the forefront of my consciousness and am addicted to the rewards that occasional excellence on my part with it bestows.

It's been so extensively written and researched that I've little useful to add, other than to remind you of the universal and cross-cultural truth that people like people who show respectful and genuine interest in them. If you're not genuinely interested in other people, best give this book to someone else who is and stick with the commute.

c. Edge

It's all very well being a glass-half-fuller *and* being fascinated by the weird and wonderful lives and thoughts of others, but if you yourself don't have something compelling to say then you're little more than a talk show host – nothing wrong of course with people who are but this book isn't designed to help you to be the next Oprah, though her level of curiosity is something we might all aspire to.

A good test is to think about what your first LinkedIn (or other professional digital platform) article might be. We're going to work on developing your digital activity quite a lot later but for now just consider what your first topic might be, assuming you're not already a celebrated author. As you'll know only too well, places like LinkedIn are full of bland, boring content seemingly designed to clumsily sell, virtue signal or boost self-importance.

Even thinking about adding to these echo chambers might have you coming out in a rash. Don't fear, I'm going to help this to be less painful, but you're going to need to give me something to work with.

What is it in your area of expertise that really gets your goat? What are the brick walls you keep seeing people walking in to? What are your more radical suggestions for solving these recurrent issues?

At time of writing, my most read LinkedIn article by far is simply called 'Leaders who are great at hiring do these three things' and suggests (among a couple of other things) that we stop asking dumb, predictable questions at interviews and instead engage in normal conversations. I've always refused to ask people when interviewing them what motivates them, where they see themselves in five years and what their weaknesses are because I'm certain that anyone with half a brain knows exactly how to game these kinds of questions – and if they don't they're probably not smart enough for me to want to hire them. And don't even get me started on 'Talk me through your resume...'

Put simply, nobody is going to pay you £2k–£4k per day for bland, generic, received-wisdom advice. You're going to need to develop the confidence and skill to publicly challenge some orthodoxies, to put your views out for scrutiny, perhaps even criticism and to, therefore, make peace with some people not ever agreeing with you.

7. Have you built and maintained a good network of former colleagues and associates?

To brutalise an old adage: be careful how you treat people on the way up as you'll very much need them when you become an independent consultant.

How do you react when you get an invite to a reunion of old colleagues from a former team/organisation? Do you even get invites to reunions? Perhaps you think they are not happening? Oh dear...

A good test here is to think about how many colleagues would give you/have given you a LinkedIn recommendation. At time of writing, I've more than 250 written recommendations on my LinkedIn profile but my most treasured are the ones from former colleagues – though I have to scroll a long way back to find them.

As you know by now, my system is based on the idea of very gently selling to people who you know or who know people you know. If you've left a trail of bodies in the wake of your career, then I'm sorry but this will be one hell of an uphill battle. If for whatever reason you've not been great at developing positive and collegiate relationships with the people you've worked with over the years, then you really better have a skill that's damn near unique and in enormous demand. In which case, why on earth are you reading this book?

For the rest of us mere mortals, we're going to need some help from some old friends.

Now, this isn't to say that you needed to have been meek and mild with everyone you've ever worked with and never had a single run-in with a colleague.

For example, one of my seven founder-customers (in fact, the best gateway contact I've ever had) was formerly an HR leader at a firm where I had been a sales leader. As you might imagine, I wasn't always hugely popular with HR colleagues, not loving what I saw then as quite a lot of time-wasting bureaucracy. She and I had very much more than our fair share of altercations, typically as a result of my youthful impatience and naivety (sorry, Jeannie), but happily we stayed friends. When I called her in my first few months of independent consultant-ism and asked if I could buy her a sandwich and get her advice, she not only agreed but shortly afterwards introduced me into an ongoing procurement process (over which she had no authority but that funnily enough the now famous Gary was a decision maker within) that resulted not only in my second multi-national client but a chain of positive events that to this day continues to benefit my business.

SUMMARY

If this chapter has you feeling a bit exhausted, even a bit intimidated, then good.

Above all else, I want this book to represent the blunt reality of what it really takes to be successful as an independent consultant. If what I've said so far puts you off, then please for the love of whatever you believe in either double down on your career or find another outlet for your entrepreneurial ambition.

Independent consulting isn't easy, it won't make you millions per year and there will be lows as well as highs.

But if you get it right – and if you're planning to read on then I'm going to help you to do just that – you'll have found your perfect why and you'll be in the very privileged position of never needing a normal job ever again.

☑ The freedom, fulfillment and, perhaps surprisingly, security that independent consulting offers is worth all the effort.

☑ Anything less than 10 years' full-time corporate experience will probably inhibit your ability to charge premium rates.

☑ Your network values most what they think you are good at.

☑   Lead every conversation with a desire to deepen the relationship rather than win a contract.

☑   Enthusiastic support in your private life is key.

☑   Being likeable is critical to your success.

☑   Be certain that your network from former lives contains the minimum number of detractors.

Get free resources on taking the first steps

The Positive Momentum Network will give you more tips and advice related to taking the first steps, along with other resources, information and support for independent consultants. Sign up for free at **www.positivemomentum.com/network**

Managing Your Exit

Avoid the Bumpy Take-off

A nother of our ultimately more successful partners actually had a false start and ended up going back to a full-time role before rejoining a couple of years later. His bumpy take-off story is an object lesson in what you need to do before you hand in your resignation letter.

This guy had what should be the perfect credentials for success. He worked his way up over 20 years from being an electrical engineer to being a board level commercial leader, very well connected and respected, confident in his field, satisfied with the level he'd reached, built up a 12-month runway of funds and wanting to find a way – with enormous support at home – to spend a little less time on late night and weekend transatlantic conference calls.

CHAPTER 4

All of the elements from the previous chapter were in place then but, even though he and I had known each other for many years before he first joined, we didn't do the pre-exit work well enough and so, whilst he enjoyed some moderate success first time around, it was far from enough to meet his needs and aspirations and so he went back to a full-time role with a small, fast growing organisation with the full intention of returning to us once we'd both done what we should have previously.

Now, if I'm honest, I thought he'd slipped through my fingers and that what I considered to be my failings would mean I'd never get him back. He's an excellent leader, the organisation he'd joined were really going places, and my fear was that he'd fuel their rocket and then quite rightly hold on to enjoy the ride. In actual fact, he very cleverly turned them into a client who he still works with to this day, together with a very wide array of clients across many different industries and all over the world.

He used his period in enforced (though very lucrative) job exile to re-educate his network and build some vital new skills that have resulted in stellar and sustained success the second time around.

The most seemingly counterintuitive element of this story is that this individual had actually spent the majority of his career in sales. He'd sold products and services worth hundreds of millions of dollars. He'd won awards and career progression from former employers for his sales prowess and yet somehow that didn't help him the first time around.

What we now know is that he rushed his network by approaching them full on with an offer to borrow rather than buy him that they were neither ready for nor widely open to.

Whether you've a sales background or not, this chapter will help to make sure you do the pre-work to ensure you don't have a forced landing shortly after take off.

MYTHBUSTERS

Independent Consulting isn't a conventional career choice and certainly not for otherwise successful people in their 40s, 50s or 60s. Whilst consulting is a highly recognised and sought out career path for top-flight graduates from red brick/ivy league universities, once you're halfway (or even further) up the career ladder you're not supposed to step off, unless of course it's to start or join the next unicorn.

What this means is that the vast majority – maybe even the entirety – of your network is going to look at you very oddly when you first suggest this path to them. It's just not normal, it's likely not what they'd want for themselves and, as a result, your thinking potentially jars with their frame of reference to the extent that they will probably initially, very gently, reject the notion by giving you the old 'sounds interesting, we'll be certain to give you a call if we need some of that' routine.

And that's where the journey ends for many people. Because the group of people that they've spent the last decade (or more) talking about career progression to don't instantly get it, they give up at the very first hurdle (which actually isn't a hurdle at all, just a gateway that takes a little patience to open effectively).

MINDSET

At the risk of re-opening Chapter 3's Pandora's box, are you sure about stepping off the career ladder and giving this a proper blast?

1. Is it the right time?

In my case several (though not all) planets aligned to make the risk of doing so acceptable. I was at a career junction. The subsidiary I'd been involved in running had been divested and I'd not been invited to go with it. Alternative internal moves were somewhat on the table, but none of them looked right for me – either in my eyes nor I suspect my employer's. A clause in my employment contract with the now divested entity offered me just about enough money to give me that 12-month runway. I was being offered that six-month, temporary non-job that generously afforded me some thinking time. I grabbed that time for the amazing gift that it was, used it wisely, never looked back and I am eternally grateful, but was my situation really so unusual?

There are moments in everyone's career journey when you can plant the seeds of a different path if you choose. Reorganisations happen with often frustrating frequency. Strategies shift. Ownership changes. Investment gets redirected. All of these tectonic moments create opportunities for a potentially cushioned exit if you're brave enough to broach it. Employment law in some parts of the world can work in your favour. In many parts of Europe, particularly, if an employer wants to enforce a role change upon you, they also have to offer you a way out and, depending on how long you've been with that organisation, that can add up to more than enough for a very well tarmacked runway, maybe even a shiny terminal or two!

2. Are you willing to use your rainy day fund?

But of course you can't make it all about landing a golden (bronze in my case) parachute. You might very well have a rainy day fund already that you're perfectly happy (well, perhaps not perfectly happy but at least willing) to use. And of course you can't wait forever to get lucky with a way out that offers a pay-off. The annoying thing about life is that the clock keeps ticking and, sooner or later, if you want something you've got to take action.

Even if you've neither an opportunity for a profitable exit or a nest egg you're willing to invest, there is plenty you can do to start getting prepared, no matter whether you plan to take the step in two months or two years.

TOOLKIT

So, let's take a look at all the steps it's prudent to take before you give your boss that letter that they probably (hopefully actually) really don't want from you.

1. One more role?

There is no magic formula of former roles that make for the perfect foundation to being a 'second chapter' Independent Consultant, but there are a few components that really help:

a. Scale leadership

Your future clients will very likely all be people leaders and if you haven't done that in your career then it's an obstacle, unless your area of expertise is very rare indeed. As you'll know if you've been one, people leadership is tricky to master and issues with it are often at the root of the problems an organisation is facing. Just knowing it academically isn't enough. We can all read books on leadership. If you haven't led a team (or even a few teams) maybe stay on the ladder just long enough to experience the pleasure and pain that is leading others in their endeavours.

b. Career diversity

Every time you change organisation – whether in the same industry or not – you get a big hit of the new. New colleagues, new cultures, new approaches, new frustrations. All of this fuels your ultimate ability to help future clients make sense of their circumstances. You'll start to see patterns. You'll develop a deeper respect for how challenging it is to run a modern organisation. You'll get new stories that will later help others with their dilemmas. Thirty years in a single organisation isn't a show-stopper but you certainly better have held a relatively wide number of roles during your extended period of incredible loyalty.

c. Taking on a challenge

Nothing quite beats experience in a role which your boss is slightly embarrassed to ask you to do. My first role at the pre-IPO telecoms company I joined in the mid-90s was a gruelling three-hour door-to-door daily driving commute, but a year later we opened a new head office that halved this and enabled me to take the train instead. After six months of getting up a little later, home a little earlier (sometimes even after a drink or two with colleagues) my boss told me about an acquisition we'd made and a role he wanted me to take with the newly acquired business. The rub? A four-hour door-to-door daily driving commute. And (though he didn't mention this initially) a group of people to lead who'd previously worked for one of the world's most established technology companies and had now been sold against their will to a bunch of telecoms mavericks. They didn't exactly roll out the red carpet for me each day that I arrived after my lovely early morning drive. Have you got a couple of tours of duty under your belt? Doesn't matter whether you brilliantly solved the challenge or just learnt a lot about how not to do it next time. Scars are as valuable as trophies in fuelling your ultimate success.

2. The 'If I did, would you?' conversation

Despite having now built my own business, I don't see myself as an entrepreneur. When we fill in those questionnaires from financial advisors, my wife and I always come out as 'moderate to low' on the risk tendency scale. That's why, back in late 2002 when we first came up with the idea that I'd abandon an apparently safe job, we both rather surprised ourselves and so immediately started coming up with ideas to mitigate the risk. One of these was to write a list of 20 or so people who I would go and ask what they thought of the idea. The list was principally comprised of trusted former colleagues, bosses and one or two friends who were in corporate jobs and who I thought might be the kind of people who sometimes hired consultants – or whatever daft thing I was calling myself at the time.

The ask of each of these people was simple and direct: if I became an independent consultant, would you hire me?

Now, of course, you can't just land this question on people without a bit of context.

I explained that I hadn't resigned yet, wasn't at risk of being fired (as far as I knew), wasn't fishing for business (at least not overtly) and certainly wasn't looking for them to tell me what they thought I wanted to hear. I reminded them each of my very young family and my wife and my preference for 5* holidays.

On that basis, and knowing how well my career trajectory had been going up until that point, most of them told me it was a stupid idea at my age and that I should either stay where I was or move to another corporate job with a big fancy title.

However, one or two were intrigued.

Being smart people they asked me lots of challenging questions before venturing an opinion. They made me squirm more than a bit with issues that I hadn't even thought about.

But then, cautiously and with plenty of caveats, they said they could see me doing it. They offered guidance, all well-meaning, some of it brilliant, some of it a little less so, but no matter – it was enough to give me the confidence to take another step toward writing the 'it's not you, it's me' letter to what turned out to be my final employer.

PRO TIP
Ask Those You Trust

Go quietly ask 20 of your most trusted contacts what they think of the idea. Give them explicit permission and encouragement to burst your bubble if they think it needs it. Don't make unanimous, or even anywhere near majority, approval your threshold for moving forward.

If this is meant to be, then this test will give you a clear signal. And if you're really lucky, you might just plant some seeds that propagate into future engagements of one sort or another.

3. Read, listen, watch

I heard a brilliant podcast recently where a banker-turned-chef reported that she'd made this major diversion in her career because a mentor who she'd turned to about feeling a little disillusioned with her current career path had asked her which section of the Sunday papers she turned to first. For her it was always something about food. Recipes, restaurant reviews, articles on nutrition. And so she discovered and very successfully pursued her true passion.

For me, it's always been the business pages. I find them endlessly fascinating and am constantly thirsty for new ideas and insights about how to do business better. Whether tales of triumph or disaster, I'm an addict for the hit of another real-world example.

Now you really don't need to be as nerdy as me about business, but you do need to read widely and pre-resignation is as good a time as any to get started if you're not already doing so.

Premium rate consultants are expected to be well read. They are expected to have credible reference points that extend beyond their own experience. They are expected to have their finger on the pulse of latest trends and new innovations. This isn't a serving suggestion. It's a core part of the recipe of success.

We're incredibly lucky to be living in what many have described as the information age. The explosion of insight, analysis – and of course a whole lot of hyperbolic bilge – is amazing and getting access to great thinking just keeps getting easier and cheaper.

Separating the wheat from the chaff isn't easy, though, and so below I offer my favourite sources that are relevant in the early 2020s:

a. Current affairs

I'm a subscriber to *Quartz* for my daily morning news fix and *The Week* for my weekly global round up. I like these two outlets because they offer a broad perspective from multiple new sources. I've learnt that it's important to be informed on all sides of the various arguments that rage around the world since the range of points of view you're likely to engage with in your new life is equally wide.

b. **Harvard Business Review**

Not a cheap subscription I'll grant you and often a little too North American-centric in its thinking, it is still pretty much the journal of record for anyone genuinely interested in the latest business thinking. I don't agree with it all, find some of it a little too academic, but after 20 years of subscribing I still scour every issue and always learn something new and brilliant.

c. **McKinsey Insights**

Like them or loathe them, McK's are regarded by most as the gold standard in the management consulting industry and in recent years they've decided to democratise their thinking and make it available for free. The quality of their writing is remarkable, the data visualisations are rich and engaging and the speed with which they keep up with the zeitgeist is impressive. Damn them!

d. **TED**

If you're more of a visual person, the free intellectual banquet that is TED just keeps getting more and more delicious. Not only can you learn how to convey often complex ideas in 18 minutes or less, but you can also get instant, on-demand access to world-class, carefully curated thinking on an incredible array of topics and from an increasingly diverse global perspective. The main problem is that watching one far too easily leads to another and before you know it several hours of binging has passed. There are however much less productive ways to while away your time.

e. Podcasts

If you're more auditory/a multi-tasker who likes to learn while mowing the lawn (that's me!) then the smorgasbord that is the world of podcasts is for you. It's impossible to recommend a single podcast series as at present new ones are appearing every day – some brilliant, some awful, some so full of ads that they drive you mad – so just dive in, don't over-think it and if you're not enjoying an episode turn it off and find another one. You'll never be short of choice that's for sure!

f. Books

Over the years I've read hundreds of business books. Correction: I've read the first chapter of hundreds of business books. Despite checking reviews and acting on recommendations from others, I still only find myself getting past chapter one in about one in three I pick up.

Just like with podcasts, it's impossible to make a single recommendation but there are a few timeless classics, all of which I've read in their entirety and most more than once, that in my view are required reading (or listening if you prefer an audiobook) for anybody serious about this profession (these are the ones that many people say they've read but often actually have not):

i.   *Good to Great* by Jim Collins

ii. *How to Win Friends & Influence People* by Dale Carnegie

iii. *The 7 Habits of Highly Effective People* by Stephen Covey

iv. *The Five Dysfunctions of a Team* by Patrick Lencioni

v.   *What They Don't Teach You at Harvard Business School* by Mark McCormack

vi. *Black Box Thinking* by Matthew Syed

vii. *Nudge* by Richard H. Thaler & Cass R. Sunstein

viii. *Outliers* by Malcolm Gladwell (plus really anything else he's written)

ix. *Dare to Lead* by Brené Brown

As important as the classics are (and of course there are hundreds more), for me the best books are the ones that tell the story of a business/businessperson. My favourites include:

i.   *Lean In* by Sheryl Sandberg

ii. *Shoe Dog* by Phil Knight

iii. *Transforming Nokia* by Risto Siilasmaa

iv. *Maverick!* by Ricardo Semler

v.   *Rework* by Jason Fried

vi. *The Ride of a Lifetime* by Robert Iger

vii. *Made in America* by Sam Walton

viii. *No Rules Rules* by Reed Hastings

4. Supersize your LinkedIn network

So you knew this was coming again, right?

If you're already at 100+ connections for every year you've been in business, *and* if you've sent a connection request or accepted one in the last 10 days, then you can skip this section.

No?

OK, so let's deal with this once and for all.

If your view is that LinkedIn is a platform overflowing with self-serving egotists putting out vacuous platitudes and (very) faintly veiled promotional messages, then by and large I'm happy to agree with you. Adopt the moral high ground and steer clear if it somehow makes you feel better. It won't make you any wealthier – indeed it will probably have the opposite effect – but at least you will have the smug satisfaction of having risen above it all.

I don't like the fact that the best connected people are the ones who most get on in life any more than perhaps you do, but it is a fact of modern existence and choosing to consciously resist it professionally simply means that you should not pursue independent consulting.

The question should not be whether being well connected or not is a good thing but instead what you can do to make the world a better place by being well connected.

I didn't go to a fancy private school or university. I didn't start out knowing anyone who could give me any kind of initial leg up in the fields I chose. Whilst of course being male and white is an unfair advantage (an injustice that all of us whitey blokes need to use our privilege to help to correct), beyond these major factors, I had no other starting position bestowed on me by others. The professional connections I made, I made by myself and when LinkedIn came along I leapt on, as it offered, really for the first time, a supercharged and democratised way of getting better professionally connected that was open to all, less intimidating/nauseating than going to some awful 'networking event' and didn't require you to know some secret handshake or own a special tie.

However, there is nothing worse than the person who suddenly invites you to connect with them on LinkedIn because their job is under threat. You haven't heard from them for bloody years and then out of the blue comes a request to connect. Grr...

So, if you haven't resigned yet (or been otherwise liberated from wage slavery), then now is the time to retrieve your LinkedIn password, accept those old connection requests from former colleagues who maybe in truth you didn't like so much and get connection requests sent to anyone and everyone you've ever worked with professionally.

Yep, *anyone and everyone* you've ever worked with.

I'm not saying you should accept random requests to connect with people you've never heard of, but I am saying that it is important that anyone you've ever been associated with professionally, however long ago and however loosely, is invited to your network.

"

*Half of your network
will never help you; the
trouble is you don't know
which half.*

"

TRAP TO AVOID
Don't Overthink Your Connection Requests

Too many people overthink and over filter. Somehow, they think there is some virtue in only being connected to people they know really well/highly respect. I just don't get it. Of course quality matters – but quantity more so. Others worry that perhaps your former boss's boss won't remember you so better not to send them a connection request at all. Huh?!?! Send the damn thing and if they don't accept, well who cares? Nothing lost.

To horribly misquote John Wanamaker: half of your network will never help you; the trouble is you don't know which half.

But being well connected is only the start.

LinkedIn (indeed networking in general) is at least as much about what you can do for others as it is about what they can do for you. Not a new or revolutionary principle but fortunately still a minority sport. I say fortunately because the few who give gener-

ously and often without expecting instant – even any – reciprocity really stand out. Later, I'm going to lay out exactly how to use LinkedIn in a way that gets you noticed for all the right reasons but for now just go and take a look at your home newsfeed and find someone in your network who is looking for help – and help them – or simply just give an encouraging reaction to something else that someone has posted.

It takes moments and can mean the world to others.

5. A little bit of light moonlighting?

On the wall in my office, alongside my picture of my founder customers and my whiteboard of client connections, is a framed picture of my very first invoice, together with the client's compliment slip and the cheque they paid with; it's not the actual cheque of course, I banked that within moments of receiving it, just a colour copy. It wasn't for a lot of money, but it means the world to me, especially as an old friend had the idea and surprised me with it. But there is one small detail that reveals the risk aversion I mentioned previously. I left my last full-time role at the end of December 2002 and yet this invoice is dated October 2002. I'd decided to leave late that summer but, since I wasn't completely out of the door, I arrogantly believed that until I'd handed in my security pass they'd still want me to stay. Since I was risking (what felt to me like) a fairly big payoff, I got written permission from my then boss to do this but remember I was in my non-job by then and so it was pretty easy for my employer to agree to this so long as I wasn't doing something for a competitor. As you can imagine the confidence boost of someone actually paying for my services was amazing and, though it hardly triggered an immediate tsunami of further invoices, it was more than enough to make me feel like this was the right path.

PRO TIP
Who Could You Help?

Are there organisations you know who don't compete with your current employer but might value what you're great at? Maybe it doesn't even involve charging them for it. The world is full of amazing not-for-profit organisations doing vital work helping to resolve some big societal issues and who are generally in desperate need of expertise, although they have no funds to pay for it. If you choose this route, you get both confidence and, in my experience, immense fulfillment. In fact, pro bono work should in my view always form a part of your practice, but more on that later.

Your version of moonlighting could, of course, simply be some quiet pre-marketing. Gary and I spent 18 months subversively plotting and planning his assured exit from his full-time job. In fact, he resigned from it just 10 minutes after I'd received a six-figure purchase order from a client for his services. To this date that remains the largest ever first contract any of our partners have ever attained. Perfect planning, ultra-low initial risk on Gary's part.

6. Join a community

I'm not talking about going off grid, wearing sandals every day and growing vegetables on an island (as fun as that might be) but rather finding like-minded groups of professionals who are either having the same thoughts as you about a possible transition to becoming an independent consultant or indeed have already done it. Networking groups abound, both on and off-line and a quick internet search will quickly reveal lots of options, some good and some truly awful, and as ever the only way to find the right ones for you is to give a few a try.

BLATANT PLUG ALERT: we've built a community website that accompanies this book. We've built it especially for people who are considering/in the early stages of becoming an Independent Consultant, and for the price of your email address you'll find tonnes of regularly updated material to help you along the way as well as means of connecting with the Positive Momentum team and even how you could become a Positive Momentum partner if you were so inclined. Head to **www.positive-momentum.com/network** and I look forward to talking to you.

SUMMARY

You cannot completely eliminate the risk of deciding to give Independent Consulting a go. However, there's plenty you can do to substantially reduce that risk. Detaching from the terminal can be scary, the runway can be bumpy (maybe even a little longer than you hoped) and the take off can be turbulent, but once you're up above the clouds, well the view is really something else.

☑ Look out for the opportunities to move your career in a different direction.

☑ Building a financial cushion is best but there are other ways.

☑ Consider whether what you are good at is a genuine passion.

☑ Ask trusted colleagues for their unvarnished advice.

☑ Become a committed and highly effective LinkedIn user.

Get free resources on managing your exit

The Positive Momentum Network will give you more tips and advice related to managing your exit, along with other resources, information and support for independent consultants. Sign up for free at

www.positivemomentum.com/network

Part 3

Setting Yourself up for Success

CHAPTER 5

Setting Up – The Early Days

Keep Learning

Sarah had been in banking for a couple of decades. She'd worked for four different well-known institutions and had ultimately been the leader of a product area, but a change in circumstances triggered the desire to find a different way of working and independent consulting got her attention as an option.

Using her well-honed skills, Sarah was forensic in her due diligence. She wanted to know exactly what needed to be done to achieve sustained success, she wanted measurable proof of the value of each of the proposed components of the formula and she wanted (indeed, still wants) to regularly review progress against all available metrics.

In other words, she asked *a lot* of challenging questions.

She was particularly curious about the apparent lack of a conventional proposition. She'd spent thousands of hours over the years with her banking clients helping them to succeed (and therefore pay back their loans) in part by focusing on better defining and then marketing their own proposition, so her uncertainty on this matter was totally understandable.

Having got enough reassurance on this to go ahead, she followed our advice and went headlong into connecting with her network under her new brand as a consultant. However, her work rate and openness in pre- and de-briefing pretty much every early meeting is something else. Always believing she can improve, she has an unquenchable thirst for pulling apart every conversation to find those marginal gains of improvement.

This super-smart mindset, together with warm, genuine and generous relationship-building skills, has enabled her to develop a phenomenal consulting practice. She put the work in in the early months and years, trusted the system and today benefits from a diverse client set that will continue to evolve and provide for her for many years to come.

"

Above all else, don't
start cold calling
people who you've no
connection with.

"

MYTHBUSTERS

Until you send that first, euphoric invoice you'll feel a natural anxiety. You'll travel to every initial meeting trying to convince yourself that it really doesn't matter what the outcome is but secretly hoping that they'll have something for you. You'll feel frustrated by the (many) meetings that don't yield a thing and you'll be walking on air after the few where there's a sniff of something. The good news is that you'll be spending all this early time talking to people who know you well already or to people who know people that you know well. You'll have plenty in common. Most of them (though I admit not all) will be warm, welcoming and want to help you. Of course plenty of them won't be able to help you directly, but you'll be amazed by the number who can help indirectly. Above all else, don't start cold calling people who you've no connection with. The level of rejection to be found on that route is something only the most hardened new business salesperson can withstand. Worse than that, for reasons we've thoroughly explored in previous chapters, with consulting it simply does not work. In fact, it damages your desired premium reputation.

MINDSET

In 1989, at the tender age of 21, on my very first day as a new business salesperson at Pitney Bowes, I was sent by my new boss (and to this day one of my best friends) to the Strand in Central London, just across the river from our decidedly unglamorous offices in an area called Elephant & Castle (which was far from as hip then as it is today). My boss had told me to do something which sounded very simple. 'All' I had to do was buzz the front door of all the businesses up and down The Strand, ask the receptionist, or whoever answered, for a compliment slip (remember them?!) and then ask whether they already had a franking machine and if not (or if they did but it was one from one of our competitors) who the office manager was.

That's it.

Get 50 compliment slips, he told me, come back to the office, call them all up and likely get 10 appointments from which I'd probably get 3 sales, shortly after which I'd be salesperson of the month, and in a year or two CEO…

(He didn't actually say the CEO bit but I'm sure it's what he meant.)

Easy, right?

Well for me, not so much.

I stood in front of the first door and froze.

What was I doing here?

Literally just weeks before I'd been bringing in the harvest, driving tractors in the countryside just like I had pretty much all my life up to this point, and suddenly I was in an ill-fitting suit, carrying a cheap briefcase and about to barge my way unannounced and uninvited into a company I knew nothing about in a landscape that was alien to me to promote a product that, in truth, I knew virtually nothing about.

I didn't buzz that first door but instead went and had a cup of tea and 'reviewed the situation'.

I seriously considered going back to the office and telling my new boss it was all a horrible mistake and that I should head back to the farm and trouble him no longer.

But I've never been a quitter and so something in me made me drink up my dodgy cuppa, get back out on The Strand and start knocking on some doors.

After several painful hours, I managed to get about 10 compliment slips.

I slunk back to the office to show my meagre efforts to my new boss – who was unimpressed to say the least. Then I called them all up, mumbling about coming to see them, and failed to book a single appointment.

As first days go, it wasn't the best.

Just as I was skulking off to head back to my bedsit in Plumstead (also decidedly unpleasant in those days) at the end of the day, my heroically patient (perhaps a bit deluded) boss told me that we were going to the pub.

Not an invitation you understand; it was an instruction.

Once ensconced in The Duke of Clarence with a pint of London's foaming best before me, my real induction slowly began.

One by one, I got to know all the other salespeople.

The geniuses, the rogues, the lifelong salespeople, the passers-through on their way to something else, all of whom generously imparted their knowledge – normally in exchange for a pint of something or other – and that's the point of this story.

Be willing to learn

I only survived – and in truth I only *just* survived those first couple of years – by learning from others and building from one client to two and then two to four and so on.

I became known for the relationships I was able to build with my clients, and then my ability to sell them something else or for them to recommend me to some-one they knew in another organisation.

For a while we had a relationship with a big photo-copier manufacturer, and I soon realised that people bought copiers much more frequently than they bought franking machines (which seemed to be basically inde-structible) and if I focused on them I could sell more to people who already knew me.

I even won a television (the manufacturer we worked with also made TVs) for being the top salesperson in the country. It had pride of place in my living room for many, many years.

129

The key to this story is the discipline I had drilled into me in those early years. The reality is that relatively few organisations either needed or wanted what I was selling – but the ones who did, really did and it was my job to find them.

I learnt to love the process of looking but fundamentally never forgot the first rule – to find a prince (or indeed princess) you need to kiss a lot of frogs.

Whilst you'll never have to ask someone you've never met before for a compliment slip, the first few months might feel like a slog – but the big difference is that you'll only be talking to people you know – or who know people that you know.

But be under no illusion, it *is* a numbers game.

The probability of finding easy early opportunities is low.

It's not non-existent but it is low.

TRAP TO AVOID

Don't Sit at Home, Get Out There!

The absolute best way to increase the probability is to get out there and start buying coffees, breakfasts, lunches, dinners, whatever it takes as often as possible.

If you've got the network and the expertise, the only other thing you need is the stamina.

The reason most people who are otherwise perfectly well qualified fail?

They simply don't get out and see enough people.

TOOLKIT

So you've done it. You're an Independent Consultant and you're open for business. What now?

Well, we need to get you announced to the world and that means our old friend LinkedIn again.

As you'll know, when someone changes their role, LinkedIn pushes that out as an automated announcement in the feed of all their contacts and it's the perfect chance to see who reacts to that as they could just be some of your early clients.

At the very least they are people to meet with.

But let's not get ahead of ourselves here.

1. Your LinkedIn profile needs a spring clean to get it Consultant Ready

Here are the keys to an appealing profile:

a. Photo

Up-to-date photo and where your face fills the frame. Most people look at LinkedIn on their mobiles these days and if you've some odd picture where your whole body is in the image, they won't see your face and that's obviously how all of those of us blessed with eyesight recognise people. You don't need some fashion shoot shot – a selfie is just fine but a blank background and zooming in on your face is key.

b. Banner

Upload something to the banner image but avoid the cheesy quotes or pixelated images that cheapen some people's brands. Download a high res image that conveys the brand you want to portray and upload that. If you can't think what that is for you for now, then leave it blank.

c. About

Write max four short sentences in your About section. Keep it simple, straightforward, factual and not overly self-congratulatory.

d. History

Tidy up your career history. Make sure all your former roles are there but limit the amount of information you've shared about each. A sentence or two is fine but detailed explanations of all your achievements... well, you should be beyond all that guff...

e. Headline

Decide how you're going to describe your new identity. You have both a Headline and your Current Position to consider. Suggest avoiding the cheesy headlines with emojis and worthy statements. Keep it simple and to the point. When I started out, I had 'Consultant – Trainer – Coach' as my headline and that seemed to do the trick.

f. Connections

Connect with anyone and everyone you know. If you're below 50 connections for each year of your career, get some invites out quickly and remember – if you're using the browser version – to add a simple personal note to each to maximise the chance of them accepting.

g. Follow

Some people (especially very big names) either prefer or only allow you to 'follow' them. Following individuals who are active on LinkedIn is another way of learning what people are thinking and being on-trend. At time of writing, following people (LinkedIn currently calls them Influencers) like Bill Gates, Richard Branson, Nancy Duarte and Ariana Huffington, to name but a very few, is de rigueur.

h. Contact Details

Update your contact details and get your email, mobile phone number and birthday on there. Anything that makes it easy for potential clients to get in touch when they need you.

i. Privacy

Relax the privacy settings. Unless you've some particular reason for needing to protect your privacy – in which case this might not be the wisest career choice

– get LinkedIn working for you by giving them permission to make it as easy as possible for people to see your profile and activity. LinkedIn has ever more creative ways of promoting you on the platform but naturally allows you to restrict these if you wish. Don't.

j. Recommendations

Ask former colleagues for recommendations. Not only is it great for your ego, but these can also be enormously helpful in referencing when potential clients are considering your services. Don't over-think who to ask. Get the invites out. Worst case they ignore the request. Of course the key here is to give recommendations as much as you receive them. Lots of 'received' but very few 'given' recommendations is not a good look...

k. Groups

There are thousands and thousands of groups on LinkedIn, most of which have been set up on a whim by someone and have relatively few members. However, the big groups are really big. The largest have 100k+ members and where the topic coincides with your interests you should definitely join. Remember that what we're seeking here is subtle visibility, don't go trying to pitch everyone or you'll soon be ejected from the club! Every group you join is another little pebble in the pond.

I.   **Newsfeed**

Engage with your newsfeed more frequently. You should be looking at your newsfeed at least once per day and regularly reacting to posts from your network either with a simple 'like' or a substantive comment: something more than 'congrats' and instead a reference to them and when you knew each other to give them that gentle relationship nudge. If people are looking for charity sponsorship, give them a donation. If they're looking for people, share it to your network. Be helpful, kind and generous.

So now you've changed your status on LinkedIn, you've got some new business cards – and little other stationery hopefully – and are looking at an empty diary.

Well, we've got to get you busy and, as I've already laboured, that means getting some meetings booked.

2. Introducing the C2C

At Positive Momentum we call any meeting (from a casual call to a quick sandwich to a full-on business meeting and everything in between) where the other person isn't paying for your time, a C2C.

It's a slightly daft acronym conceived by a fondly remembered former partner and it stands for Coffee to Cash. It's become a mainstay of our lexicon because it's so important and it's THE leading indicator of our success.

We measure and monitor this KPI more than any other metric in our business.

In fact, the geekiest (and uncoincidentally the most successful) amongst us, track this KPI alongside several others on our personal dashboards – see below. Think of this like your health app on your phone tracking all of your practice's 'vital signs'.

POSITIVE ●
MOMENTUM

Maximising Visibility	
Average weekly C2C's*	7.80
Average weekly LinkedIn network growth*	5
Average weekly LinkedIn SSI*	72
Average weekly articles/books sent in post*	1.50

Turning Contacts into Contracts	
Number of new proposals in last 4 weeks	4
Number of live opportunities in pipeline	15
YTD conversion of C2C's to contracts	11.8

Delivering Distinctively		
YTD average value of a contract	£	14,578
Average Day Rate over last 12 months**	£	3,275
YTD number of phase 4 clients		5
YTD number of phase 5 clients		7

* average of last 4 weeks

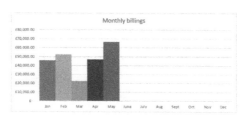

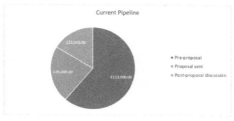

We know that if the average number of C2Cs per partner per week drops below five, we'll likely have some revenue dip in three to six months' time. However, what we also know is that if it exceeds 15 we'll also likely have a revenue dip in two to four months' time.

As I said before, this *is* a numbers game, but that doesn't mean that more and more makes things better and better.

After nearly two decades of monitoring, we've found the sweet spot and whilst of course the month-to-month pattern varies wildly depending on the intensity of projects a particular consultant is engaged in, we know that the quarterly and certainly half year C2C trends are absolute predictors of success.

In the next chapter, we'll talk in detail about the anatomy of a great C2C, but for now let's just focus on how to get lots of them in your schedule.

A classic failure in this respect is to blast out the same spammy email to everyone in your contact list. So many people I've worked with have done this and it's an incredibly difficult genie to put back in the bottle. You can't unsend it and anything that comes after will be blighted by the clumsiness of this initial approach.

If you've already done this, don't panic.

It's not irretrievable.

In fact you might have had some 'success' from it. Maybe one out of the 100 you sent it to came back to you and maybe you even secured some work.

Great news (kinda) but 1:100 isn't going to work long term. Instead, follow these steps:

Step 1

Make a BIG list of who you want to have a C2C with.

A simple spreadsheet is useful for keeping track of this – something that will be especially helpful when you start getting someone else to manage your diary, more of which later.

You don't need to go full CRM with this.

You'll likely spend more time setting that up than you should and not get out C2Cing.

Make the longest list you can and don't worry about whether you think someone is a 'decision maker' (whatever they are) or not.

PRO TIP
Be Open-minded About Meeting Anyone

As I've said before, lots of people you will C2C with will be gateway contacts and seeing plenty of them at whatever level they are is generally infinitely more valuable than talking your way into a coffee with a Fortune 500 CEO who just happened to be a former colleague 'back in the day'.

Step 2

Do some research.

What we're seeking here is something topical happening with the individual and/or their organisation.

There is nothing more damaging to your shiny new consultant creds than discovering something major is happening with their organisation and that's in the public domain *after* you've contacted them about booking a C2C.

Obviously, take a glance at their website and the person's LinkedIn profile. That's 101 stuff no matter how well you think you know them. But if that does not yield anything topical then web search both the individual and their organisation, maybe even their industry if you're struggling.

Google offer a fantastic free service called Alerts **https://www.google.co.uk/alerts**, which allows you to monitor the web for any word or words on an ongoing basis. Personally, I track around 40 organisations/individuals (that I refresh monthly) and get a single weekly digest email with the top three news stories that relate to each. I've long since lost track of the number of times I read something here that offered me a pretext for getting back in touch with someone and that then led to an engagement.

Let's be clear here – I'm not spending hours on this. Once I've found my topical hook, my research for this phase is done. If that comes in 30 seconds then great.

If we secure the C2C, we'll do much more, but for now I just want something to open with.

Step 3

Craft your email/LinkedIn invitation message.

Brevity is the key here.

No one is interested in reading some long message about what you're up to.

Remember, what appeals most to everyone is themselves and so your very first sentence – and ideally the subject line if an email – should be all about them.

This is why your Step 2 research really matters.

Whatever you've discovered you should refer to up front and then get straight to the point. Something like the following works well:

SUBJECT: TIKTOK ZEBRAS

Hi Mark and hope you're well.

Many congratulations on the Cannes Lions award for the Accelerate campaign last month. The judges really seemed to be impressed by the digital component – those TikToks with the Zebras are so clever – and I recall that as always being close to your heart.

I am in Atlanta for meetings with clients on 23rd October and then again on 2nd November. Which of those would suit you best for a coffee and a catch up?

Looking forward to seeing you soon,
Matt

PRO TIP
Crafting The Right Message

▶ *Never use boring, lazy subject lines like 'Meeting' or worse 'Follow Up'. Give it inbox appeal by making it about them, without of course being a cheesy spam-meister.*

▶ *First lines should have specificity and continue to be all about them. Let them know you're noticing them by playing back some triumph they've recently had. Flattery works but take it easy as there's a fine line between that and sycophancy.*

▶ *DO NOT ask whether, perhaps, if it's not too much trouble and of course it really won't take long, they might find a few minutes for you – if it's not too much trouble, of course I know you're very busy. Asking them for time has a 50:50 (at best) chance of success and I don't like those odds.*

▶ *Instead, assume that they will want to see you and offer two dates to choose from. That's dates not days. If I ask you what you're doing next Wednesday you might try to remember, whereas if I ask* what you're doing on the 16th, it acts like a mental nudge to increase the probability of you opening your diary, potentially before you've even considered whether you want to see me.

▶ How you choose the dates matters too. The first date should be more than one week away. Why? Because if you're free tomorrow (and in the early days you probably will be) then this consulting thing probably isn't going quite as well as you're suggesting. Equally, busy people are, well busy, and so there is little chance of them having a window in the next week anyway.

▶ The second date should be in another week and on another day of the week. In another week because they might have vacation or a week-long commitment. On another day because you might have hit a recurring meeting day with your first choice.

▶ So what if they reply saying they can't do either of those? Well, hallelujah. We're now discussing 'when' not 'if' and you can easily go back with another pair of dates (no slipping back to single dates or worse asking them when it might suit them and losing all control). Of course, you can't continue that ad infinitum, but most people will eventually concede and offer you something.

This might all seem a bit detailed for a simple meeting request email, but I promise you that if you don't master this game all other bets are off. These techniques are designed to progressively increase the probability of getting those all-important first meetings – and plenty of them.

Step 4

Keep busy...

As someone who previously had a level of seniority, I guess you're accustomed to people replying to your emails pretty quickly? That might not quite be the case with these invites...

After you've clicked send on your brilliantly crafted C2C invitation and the minutes turn into hours and the hours into days as you wait for a reply if you're not careful, you'll start running all sorts of self-defeating programmes.

Prevent this malaise by connecting with more old friends on LinkedIn, sending more invitations, reading more articles, going for a run, mowing the lawn, baking bread, going to the pub; essentially, anything other than constantly refreshing your inbox.

Of course, some people won't reply. Who cares? Their loss.

You've expertise, a finite inventory (remember no. of days you want to bill per year?) and the reality, even if you worked seven days per week, is that there is simply no way you could serve the needs of everyone in your net-work if they all said, 'Yes, come on in'.

Of course, some people will reply instantly. And I bet they'll be the ones you procrastinated over sending a meeting invite to for the longest.

Years of experience with hundreds of rookie consul-tants has shown that the contacts you feel most nervous about contacting turn out to be the ones who value you the most.

The moral of this story: opportunities propagate in the most unlikely corners of your network. Judge less and book more meetings...

SUMMARY

Many leaders talk about the importance of the first 100 days in a new role and it couldn't be more true of setting up as an independent consultant too.

The habits you form in those first few months will serve or cost you for many years to come.

You might 'get lucky' and score an early client. Whenever a new Positive Momentum consultant wins work in the first few weeks of launching their practice, I feel both joy and fear. Joy because the confidence boost is always worth way more than the gig. Fear because it might stop them putting the work into opening many, many more lines of enquiry.

I'm certain I've irritated countless new colleagues by nagging them about their next client just seconds after they've announced they've secured their first engagement.

As Andy Grove, the founder of Intel, famously said: *'Success breeds complacency, complacency breeds failure, only the paranoid survive.'*

☑ Don't waste your time or energy on approaching people who neither know you nor know people who know you.

☑ The absolute key to success is the number of people you get out and see.

Get free resources on setting up your practice

The Positive Momentum Network will give you more tips and advice related to setting up your practice, along with other resources, information and support for independent consultants. Sign up for free at **www.positivemomentum.com/network**

CHAPTER 6

In the Initial Meeting

Charm and Disarm

When I first met one of my now longest standing Positive Momentum colleagues, Jamie, I was a cocky young sales director, fresh at the telecoms firm, whose ultimate fate you might recall from Chapter 1.

Our first meeting (many years before the nice man from PWC arrived unannounced) involved me being rather cross about an idea a marketing agency (of which my now colleague was at the time a co-owner) had presented to us.

My ever patient and professional marketing director peer had (foolishly as it turns out) invited me into a meeting with the agency to review the idea, where thankfully Jamie was present. Rather than arguing with the uninformed and irrational objections of someone who was clearly just trying to make an immature mark on the space,

Jamie instead worked his magic with me – something I've since been lucky enough to have a ringside seat to him doing with others many times since.

First, he'd really done his homework.

He'd heard about me (and my voluble opinions) and so had looked into my professional background, spoken to some of my team and came armed with insights about us, some of which I was previously unaware of and all of which I hadn't actually expected him to know.

As soon as he arrived, he was in full disarm mode.

I've no doubt we childishly kept them waiting and yet when we summoned them Jamie was full of smiles and welcome, mentioning quickly that moving from AT&T (where he said he'd heard I'd been having success 😬) to this firm must have been a big decision but that someone like me was exactly what this business needed.

And you know what?

I fell for it.

Hook, line and sinker.

Where I'd gone in ready to let them have it, instead, I quickly became like putty in their hands. I still wasn't happy with the idea, but it soon became obvious that Jamie didn't give a damn about selling the idea (he later also agreed that it was terrible!) as he'd come along for an entirely different purpose.

The relationship was what mattered to him, and he followed a charming welcome and flattering early comments with some really substantive questions that made my colleagues and me really think about what we were trying to achieve.

And so began a partnership that fuelled both a huge amount of commercial growth as well as some incredible fun together.

Today Jamie is one of our most successful consultants and, whilst he's got more than enough marketing expertise under his hood, it's his ability to make clients like him, as well as respect him, that is his real superpower.

Having expertise certainly matters but if you don't also know how to create affinity with others then, as we've already explored, there really are easier ways of making money.

MYTHBUSTERS

The goal is not opportunities (the harder you look, the less you find) as people won't want to meet you again if you're too pushy.

We often say that prospective clients are like children and animals: they can smell fear.

When you're first building your practice this fear manifests as desperation for an engagement – sometimes rabidly desperate. This desperation can even be fed by the people we're meeting who innocently ask us what we're doing now and how they can help. These are massive danger zones that we're going to traverse in this chapter.

We define a C2C as a meeting, call or conversation that in any way broadens your network or deepens a relationship.

You might want to read that again.

These are NOT sales meetings. They are NOT a place for you to pitch what you think you're great at. The primary goal is NOT to win an engagement.

Now I appreciate this might be mashing the cogs a little. You might be thinking that surely by now we should be pushing our services, if only just a little. Well yes, but only a very little and only if the conditions are absolutely right.

No one is under any illusion that these meetings don't ultimately have a commercial purpose, but when you're a new consultant – in fact, even if you've been at it for years – being needy is a very big turn off and clumsy initial meetings can cut off a branch of your future client network before it's even had the chance to grow.

However, if you get these meetings right, your network will flourish and serve you for many, many years to come.

MINDSET

Don't be choosy

Most of the C2Cs I do – and I do between 250 and 300 per year – yield nothing in terms of revenue.

I meet everyone from fresh new grads through to upcoming managers and all the way to board members.

I meet people who are looking for a new role and people who are retired.

I meet people who are also consultants and people who are selling things totally unrelated to what we do.

I meet people who think consultants are all blood-sucking parasites and people who think we're the answer to everything.

Much to my EA's consternation, I never decline a meeting with anyone.

My accountant has long since given up trying to make sense of my expense account.

From egg and chips in a roadside cafe through to seven course dinners in Michelin starred restaurants, I always pick up the tab and am more than happy to meet people at a time and in a place that most suits them.

In fact, there was one time I didn't actually pick up the tab but learnt an amazing lesson:

In the early years of my business I'd been coaching a talented young marketing professional in Dublin who was working for a very famous energy drinks brand. I suspect you know the one...

At one particular session she told me that my approach reminded her of her father and that she would love to introduce us as she was sure we would get on well. I was, of course, flattered and when she told me what he did I was very interested indeed to meet him.

He was the CEO of a major division of a very large food ingredients manufacturer and spent most of his time flying around the world visiting his local factory teams and major clients and partners.

Getting time in his diary was anything but easy but I persevered for several months until we found an evening where he was travelling from the North of England to the South and had decided to stay over halfway in Warwick, funnily enough not far from where I was born.

I found an excuse to be there (I think I told him I was working with a client down the road!) and checked into the hotel at the same time as him.

We agreed to go to a Japanese restaurant that he'd already researched (typical of him as it turns out) and had a tremendous evening. Whilst of course I'd done my research on him and his firm and had plenty of (what I hoped would be good) questions to ask, by the end of the evening I rather felt that I'd had much more value from the evening than he had.

As always in such situations, I asked for the bill and was in the process of paying when he insisted that he wanted to pay. Even then I was pretty adept at brushing off requests like that, but this guy was 20 years my senior and had that look in his eye that made clear this wasn't a polite suggestion.

Not only did he pick up the tab, but as he was doing so he told me that he wanted me to send him an invoice for €1k for my time. I protested mightily but the look returned to his eye and so I resolved to let it go, never having any intention of actually sending the invoice. We said our farewells that evening as he was back on the road very early the next day enroute to Heathrow and another country.

The very next day my EA got an email from his EA saying that we'd had a very productive evening and an invoice was expected for my time. His EA explained that he believed I wouldn't send the invoice if he didn't insist (he turned out to be a mind reader too), and he would be most offended if we didn't and even included a Purchase Order number on the email.

We duly sent the invoice and so began an amazing relationship, which has included some fascinating engagements with his firm (and many others to whom he recommended me) as well as some of the best mentoring I've had in my career.

To be clear, I've never again been asked by a prospective client to bill them for our first meeting, but what I learnt that evening in Warwick eating Japanese food is that *truly committing attention and interest to someone talking about their challenges and opportunities, without explicit ulterior motive, is much more valuable than I'd previously understood.*

John told me that the space and time to talk through some important issues with an independent party was the most valuable few hours he'd had in a long time. What he taught me that evening has become core to our operating system and he's yet another person I cannot thank enough.

If you start being choosy about who you will and won't meet, if you're the kind of person who won't go out of their way to meet people where the purpose seems vague and if you don't like picking up the tab, then I say again this life isn't for you. However, if you can get your head around that Goldman Sachs principle of being 'long term greedy', if you get a kick out of meeting lots of different people in different situations, maybe even helping some of them – sometimes for money, often not – and if you know how to make people like you, then you're going to LOVE this life.

TOOLKIT

So, let's finally get into the anatomy of a really great C2C.

1. Research

As you'll have worked out by now, I'm a preparation obsessive. Not because I'm somehow an incredibly diligent person – former teachers and bosses will tell you that – but because I know I've missed opportunities by not being properly prepared, and that really hurts! All that time invested in boosting my visibility and getting the damn appointment flushed down the toilet by laziness and overconfidence.

The research you do before a C2C is THE key to a conversation that is both expansive *and* amplifies your credibility. In short, it maximises the probability of something coming up in conversation that you can help with.

Of course, researching publicly listed firms is much easier than privately owned ones. The ever-increasing degree of disclosure demanded of organisations on the public markets creates a treasure trove of information, perfect for pre-C2C planning.

Find the 'Investor' area of their website and if you love business like me, then prepare to geek out. I especially love strategy decks from events like Capital Markets days, though even quarterly earnings reports frequently include juicy morsels once you've (probably) skipped over all the accountant speak.

One of my former clients is (at time of writing) the CEO of a FTSE100 hospitality and hotels giant and whenever she and I meet for lunch (in one of the pubs they own) I always have a well-read printed copy of their latest report visible on the lunch table. She always notices, grins benevolently at my efforts, indulges a few of my questions before gently edging me back to friendly conversations about family and former colleagues. She has a clear sense of what she thinks I'm good at and will hire me again when/if she wants to. By always reading their excellent decks and reports, I make sure that when/if that day arrives I'll be on point. Until then I always enjoy our lunches, learn a great deal and am privileged to be able to call her a friend.

If an organisation is privately owned or a government department of some sort, the research can be more challenging but the aim is the same: to find out things they might not have expected you to know prior to a catch up meeting.

Whether public or private, plumb the depths of their website to find information that others are probably not getting to. Perhaps new products, new markets, new staff, new partnerships or recent awards/accreditations. Anything that will prove you went to some effort but not so much that you spent hours and hours.

Other important searches include:

▶ Google (other search engines are available) the person you're meeting.

Yes, even if you've known them for 20 years.

A Positive Momentum colleague was once frustrated that I made him do this for someone he'd known his whole life only to discover that the week before he'd done a speech at his old school. He later admitted that his old friend was very flattered he'd noticed and that it made for a much more productive conversation.

Checking out their latest tweets, LinkedIn posts and any other professional social media activity can tell you a lot about what's on their mind right now, though for the more social media addicted it might only be a picture of their lunch...

▶ Google searching the organisation and then refining by looking at the news in recent date order. Perhaps their website isn't up to date with their latest news. Perhaps an industry commentator has made some observations about them. Perhaps there is some recent research comparing them to their competitors. Whatever it might be, it might just be the line of enquiry that leads them to coughing up where they could need help.

All of this detective work is intended to help you write down five questions that will both prove that you've done your homework but also might just get them thinking about their issues in a new way. Much more on how vital these very special questions might prove to be shortly.

Over time you'll get quicker and quicker at this investigative work; in the early days of your practice you might expect to spend upwards of 45 mins on your sleuthing, whereas these days I'm generally down to about 15 mins.

We're not trying to become experts in them and their business. We want just enough knowledge to be dangerous.

2. Location

Now, of course we're always happy to go and visit clients in their fancy-schmancy offices, or increasingly in an online setting on a platform of their choosing, but how about meeting them somewhere a little different?

Those of us in Positive Momentum based in the UK often do our C2Cs at a club in Central London. Nothing flashy or ostentatious you understand, it's just a slightly different location where we can be the host, get someone out of their normal environment and pick up the tab for a very nice cup of coffee or even some great food if they've time.

These kinds of clubs are increasingly popular in cities all over the world and membership of the less show-offy ones is surprisingly affordable. It adds polish to what you're doing and is typical of consultants who are more premium in their pricing – and the sooner you can establish that principle the better, for reasons we've already explored.

If that's not for you or the client isn't based near your club, then how about an eatery near their office? As busy as everyone is, it's certain they all still eat and so why not with you? I've bought thousands of breakfasts, lunches and dinners over the years, at the full range of restaurants from fast food to haute cuisine – and have learnt to make healthier choices, especially when I've a day of all three, which isn't as rare as you might imagine. There is something about 'breaking bread' with someone that creates a different, more convivial and often much more open conversation.

I even try to control how I sit relative to the person I'm meeting. It's often not possible, of course, but if I can then I want to sit at a right angle to them rather than face to face, interrogation style. In restaurants that often involves me getting there earlier and begging for a table for three or four rather than being stuck on the row of tables for two. It's really why I prefer to eat with people at my club where they are very used to my funny seating proclivities.

3. First few minutes

Because you're meeting with people who know you, or who know people that you know, then you'll likely quickly and easily drop into friendly conversation. Indeed, this might include updating on family, common hobbies and interests, current affairs, even old colleagues/past glories.

And this is our first danger zone...

So long as the other party is very evidently comfortable in the semi-social catching-up discussion – with them doing most of the talking – then fine, but the second you notice their interest in this even slightly waning, it's time to gently unleash some of your research and use it as the basis for your first business oriented question.

PRO TIP
Get Your Notepad Ready

Always have your notepad (with your five questions) and something from their website printed out and on the table, either before they arrive/get it out as soon as you sit down. There's nothing worse than trying to surreptitiously get these out of your bag 15 minutes into the conversation when you realise you're being briefed on a possible project.

Ideally, you want to get in with this before they ask you the question we all fear – 'so what are you doing these days?' or variants on that theme.

Some of the more useless books I read on becoming a consultant suggested that what I needed for these moments was an 'Elevator Pitch': an incredible 90-second speech that would so beguile the other party with my magnetic capabilities that they would be practically begging me to work with them.

Complete nonsense, of course.

This is someone who knows you – either directly or through someone else.

They already have their own view on what they think you're good at and no amount of cheesy propaganda will do anything to change that. Indeed, if it's at odds with what they think you're good at then you're off to a very bad start.

How about something like this instead?

'I'm just doing what I was doing for one organisation for multiple organisations at the same time. Anyway, tell me about...'

Yes, it's a bit evasive – and that's the point.

It's way too early in the conversation to start narrowing down their view of what you do. That was my biggest mistake in my early years with my silly proposition. The opportunities I missed don't bear thinking about...

No, what we want to do is have a convivial conversation that is as expansive as possible to offer you the greatest range of their ailments for which they might eventually come to consider you the cure. So that means getting into questions that show you've done your research as soon as you can.

Questions like:

'I noticed the announcement about your new sales agent in Hanoi. What is it about Vietnam that attracts you?'

Nothing too clever at this point. Be sure, of course, that it's something they will know about. Don't be a smart alec and risk humiliating them with something that you know and they don't. Not a good look. Instead, do your homework about stuff you think they will be really proud of and then let them go. No need to show off your expertise just yet, just get them talking and encourage them to tell you more about how brilliant their plans are.

Now, if you're lucky they'll start to reveal the challenges they face – and let's be clear, nothing is ever perfect in business life – but they might not be ready for that kind of disclosure yet and so may well just continue to talk about all of their triumphs.

Let them.

Listen closely.

Be authentically curious.

Make notes of jargon, product names, peoples' titles, anything that's their specific company language – playing back this language accurately might be rocket fuel in the next few minutes/hours/weeks. So many uses for this that we're going to explore very soon.

But for now, relax, focus and follow their train of thought until something that's not quite so peachy reveals itself...

Now, maybe they won't perjure themselves the first time you have a meeting with them in your new identity. Some people resist telling consultants what their problems are for fear they might try to sell them a solution. Imagine that...

Seriously, consultants don't enjoy a universally positive reputation and so a little hesitancy in revealing their darkest secrets is understandable. It's why I developed a technique called Bloody Good Questions (BGQs) and it's the single most powerful element of our entire Operating System. Master this and I couldn't give a damn what your LinkedIn profile pic looks like, you'll be made.

4. The BGQ

It's our modern business take on the ancient skill of Socratic Questioning and in our experience it's the approach that makes all the difference when it comes to leading, selling, consulting and just about any other multi-person business (maybe even life) activity you can think of.

In essence, it's the ability to be able to make another human being stop and think because of what you ask rather than what you tell.

Consider your best friend or maybe the best boss or mentor you've ever had. Were they/are they great at asking you just the right question at just the right time? Is it sometimes a bit maddening that they're so on point? But do you end up appreciating them even more because of this seemingly magical ability? Of course you do.

I first used the expression BGQ back in 2003 in my very first year of consulting.

You might recall from Chapter 1 that in the final phase of my final full-time role I was given a non-job helping relationship managers in a very large bank to become better at winning new business. Whilst I knew a fair bit about how to win new B2B business, I knew next to nothing about banking, as my former employer, fortunately only later, discovered!

I realised I'd have my work cut out with experienced bankers who generally have very little patience with so-called 'soft skills experts' from outside their industry.

In preparation, I went out on the road with some of them to see how they engaged with clients in the real world and guess what I discovered? Total professionals with very impressive – in many cases market leading – expertise in their markets.

And that was their biggest problem.

I remember vividly one meeting with a potential new manufacturing client in the West Midlands of the UK when the c.30-year-old Relationship Manager opened up the discussion not with a question but by announcing that he was 'a specialist' in manufacturing – it must have been true as it was printed on his business card! The c.60-year-old MD reclined in his well-worn leather chair and with a mischievous smile on his face said, 'Well, I've been in manufacturing for 40 years, but hey why don't you tell me all about it?'

The meeting went downhill from there as the flustered, and on any other day excellent, Relationship Manager tried in vain to row back from this very bad start, but suffice to say we didn't leave that day – or indeed any subsequent day – with a mandate...

Someone once said that Knowledge is knowing the right answer whereas Intelligence is knowing the right question. Whilst I'd found my opening, I realised that I'd need something catchier and more direct than Socratic Questioning and something a lot more advanced than Fisher Price-level open and closed questioning, and so the BGQ was born.

The (mild) profanity and daft acronym is intended to make it memorable and it seems to have worked. A few years ago a guy came up to me in Schiphol Airport, of all places, and said, 'Hey, you're the BGQ guy'. He had no idea what my name was or where he'd met me, but he'd remembered BGQs – and that was more than good enough for me!

My colleagues and I not only use this technique in every C2C we do, but we've also taught this technique to thousands of businesspeople in hundreds of organisations all around the world and in countless situations, and we love particularly how we're able to use it to solve real dilemmas for clients and never just as an abstract principle.

So how can you become a BGQ pro?

▶ **As I suggested earlier, use your research to prepare five questions before every meeting.**

For a short time in the late 1990s I worked directly for the billionaire son of a 20th century perfumery legend. Our first one-on-one was at a very, very posh London hotel called Claridge's (where else?), and I sat nervously waiting for him in the lounge with my notepad open to a blank page. We spoke about the project I was leading for around 20 minutes and it seemed to go pretty well. At the end he gave me both a compliment and a criticism. He liked my energy but not my blank notes page. He suggested that whenever I meet anyone in future – billionaire or not – I should have prepared three to five questions for them and for these to be visible to both parties as a note of both respect and intent. Never forgotten that one. Thanks RSL.

▶ **Stop trying to solve everything immediately.**

In your former life as a business leader it probably often felt like being on the reception desk of an A&E department, where you needed to triage everything the minute it landed. Too many businesspeople, especially people leaders, are in a raring hurry to solve every challenge thrown their way immediately, in some delusional attempt to either get everything done or show just how clever and important they are. Being a problem solver is certainly an important skill, but it's overrated in my view. As my wife often reminds me, just because she chooses to tell me about the odd less than stellar day doesn't mean she wants all my ideas about how to make it better next time! Patience, empathy and the odd question to show you're actually listening is more appreciated than you (and too often still I) might imagine…

► **Get hypothetical.**

BGQs take a person to a place in their conscious-ness that they hadn't gone before – or were maybe even trying to avoid. Questions like 'If you could go back in time and do this all again how would you do it differently?' or 'If you had unlimited resources what would you do?' can have a surprisingly mer-curial effect.

► **Use people's own phrases when you pose questions.**

If you really want to show someone you're listening to them, playing back their own words in the form of further enquiry somehow ignites new thoughts in their head in the most remarkable way. It's especially helpful if what you're asking is a little more challeng-ing. The flattery of playback (if genuine and careful-ly delivered) can be a fantastic anaesthetic for the landing of a question that has just a little bite.

My favourite BGQ story involves my eldest daughter when she was just four and a half years old – around the time I was first developing the BGQ concept in client work.

She had only been at 'proper school' for around four weeks and one day I was at home in the afternoon, so I went to collect her in the car as the school was a few miles away.

On the way back home I asked the classic parental question of kids after school: 'What did you do today?'

Now as most parents know, there are some classic child answers to this, like 'nothing' or 'can't remember' but my little girl said something different that really landed the importance of BGQs with me.

Somewhat forthright from a very early age, she said 'Daddy, don't ever ask me that question again!' 😳

Clearly her mother and I were already becoming repetitive, and she called me on it right there and then.

She was right.

It's a terrible question.

'OK Charlotte,' I said, 'what was the best thing that happened at school today?' And you know what happened?

She thought for a moment, told me about something funny that happened with one of her new friends and we laughed and chatted about it all the way home.

Sadly, I messed up this brief triumph by lazily using the same question for the next few weeks until she said – and I suspect you're ahead of me here – 'Daddy, don't ever ask me that question again'.

You see, BGQs only really happen in the moment. They are best when based directly on something you know really matters right now to the other party. They are, therefore, only possible when you're listening to someone with totally committed intent.

Turns out they knew what they were talking about, those ancient Greek philosophers.

So, how do you know if you've asked a BGQ?

Well, of course what's most likely is that they pause and think for a moment, but what I pray for in a C2C are six magical words that if I can get a potential client to say them, then I know I'm well on the way to getting an actual engagement:

'That is a very good question.'

I genuinely still feel a thrill when a client utters these words.

(I know, I need to get out more!)

I almost want to high five myself – awkward in a meeting, even on video, I'll grant you, so I try to stay cool.

All good then, but there's actually another danger zone at this point.

The self-satisfaction of having validated your genius with a rock star question can easily give way to you showboating your knowledge in this domain and taking over the talking. Not that I've ever done that, you understand, but I've heard it's possible...

The trick here is to maintain your composure, listen harder than ever and see what comes next. All being well, all of the efforts you've made so far will be rewarded with an issue being revealed that might just be the spark from which you can carefully light the flame of an engagement.

5. Stories sell

Having heard about an issue that you believe you can help with, you've two choices:

You can either put your hand up like the over-keen kid at the front of the class and tell them that you can solve it for them or...

...you can tell a quick anecdote about a time when you were involved in the resolution of a similar issue – either during your corporate career if you're still in the early stages of practice build, or from another engagement if you've been at this consulting thing for a while.

Each year we hold a client event in aid of a British charity called The Prince's Trust. We invite three CEOs to share their experience and engage in candid conversation with an intimate, invite-only audience. The pragmatism of their counsel is always amazing. It's like getting all the juice from three business biography books in a single morning.

A few years ago one of our speakers was an amazing tech entrepreneur called Tom who brought the house down when he told us what his wife said when he'd been nominated as one of the most powerful black people in the UK: 'You're not even one of the most powerful black people in this house!'

He's an incredible storyteller and he revealed to us the beautifully simple secret to his storytelling technique, and it's something we've used ever since. It's especially useful just after you've finally got a potential client to reveal an issue that they are facing but perhaps don't quite yet associate you with being the solution.

As Tom taught us, all great stories have three components:

1. A Dragon

In our case that's the issue that we/a former client faced. The more fire breathing the dragon the better of course, but don't go over the top – this isn't panto.

Something like: '*I can really relate to that* <the issue they just shared>, *when I was at the Okey Cokey Company we had some serious issues with siloed functions to the extent that both client NPS and employee engagement rates were declining.*'

2. A Knight

The weapons you used to fight the dragon. Don't go on and on here. Just the briefest sprinkling of self-effacing fairy dust is what we're looking for. All we're doing is putting some bait on the water to see if they might nibble.

Something like: '*We started out by getting all of the managers together much more often and having carefully facilitated conversations between them. We then got an external independent professional to do some development with them both individually and as a group.*'

3. Happily Ever After

This is what happened after the dragon had been slayed. Specificity really counts here. Give them something easy to remember and, therefore, easy to retell to others.

Something like: *'Within six months of this work our client NPS had gone up by 5 points and at the end of year Employee Engagement in the previously siloed functions had gone up by 10 points.'*

Now, don't expect a standing ovation after what you'll think was a gripping yarn.

Instead, watch closely for any glimmers of interest.

All being well, you'll get some follow-up questions and, again, if you do, don't bang on. Keep dripping a little more substance out and then calibrate frequently to see how closely this experience relates to their situation.

Just like fishing, strike too early and they'll be off into the deep long before they were really on the hook.

Stay patient and keep slowly reeling them in with more BGQs and stories until they ask whether you can help. Now they might not ask directly or immediately. Some might even think stuff like this is beneath you.

Take your time.

Perhaps this isn't the thing they end up paying you to help them with. Perhaps it's just a small gateway to another, bigger conversation on another day. Remember you're trying to build opportunities for the short, medium

"

Just like fishing, strike too early and they'll be off into the deep long before they were really on the hook.

"

and long term. Not everything needs to lead to an instant engagement.

Of course, your story might very well fall completely on its derrière. If they ask you nothing about it, then you'll know.

No problem. Dust yourself off, choose another of your five questions and head off in another direction until time's up.

6. Next steps

The most common outcome of an initial C2C is a good conversation but no immediate opportunity, and you've got to view this as positive progress. These are early chess moves in a game that might take many months or even years to come to fruition.

Who cares? You practised your C2C skills, learnt something about how another organisation functions and will no doubt be welcomed back for another interesting conversation in a few months.

Plenty more fish in the sea (not sure where all these fish have suddenly come from?!).

On the other side of the equation entirely, you'll occasionally get the outcome of a red hot, immediate opportunity. It'll feel to you and the client like amazingly fortuitous timing (that's why I advocate doing lots of C2Cs – as Gary Player said, 'The harder I try, the luckier I get').

Wherever the outcome is between these two extremes, the following can be useful cards to play in making flames from embers.

▶ If you run out of time but there seems to be something there, then simply suggest a follow-up meeting in the near future. If they're wriggly then it's a good signal that they were just being polite.

▶ If it's obvious that it's something warmer then suggest a follow-up meeting that brings in other actors from their side. Issues inevitably have a number of stakeholders so another good temperature test is to see if they'll let you meet some of their colleagues to discuss it further.

▶ My favourite test of how real an opportunity is is to suggest signing a Non-Disclosure Agreement. Most organisations have a boilerplate NDA and I've signed literally hundreds of these over the years. I don't worry about the content of them, I simply want the client to feel reassured that their secrets are safe with me. I'd estimate that around four out of every five NDAs I sign turn into real engagements.

TRAP TO AVOID
Don't Celebrate Too Soon

Being in the right place at the right time is easier to achieve than many think but having found yourself with what looks like an open goal in front of you, keeping your composure before you strike the ball is critical.

If I had a pound for every C2C where I left with what felt like a sure thing in my back pocket only to lose it in the coming weeks, well, I'd have quite a few pounds.

7. Follow up email

It will be no surprise to you by now to learn that I'm fastidious about sending a carefully crafted email follow up for each and every C2C I do. Whether it was a BGQ-filled lovefest or the equivalent of a difficult first date, everyone gets a thank you and a short playback of what we discussed.

Not sure whether I do this because my mum always made me send written thank you notes after parties when I was a kid, but what I can say is that I've been surprised by the reaction on more than one occasion – many more.

Now be prepared for what I'm going to advocate here.

My style is to playback what they told me but, of course, in a synthesised manner. I want them to see that I really listened. I use their language throughout – as you might recall from the C2C invite email.

Here's a real example of something that was lukewarm at the end of the C2C and then turned into a real engagement within two weeks:

SUBJECT: £12M/MONTH BY 2025

Hi Bob and thanks again for your time yesterday. Fascinating to learn more about xyz Inc and great to see you in such fine spirits.

The story of how xyz Inc has developed to where it is today is both inspiring and instructive for all entrepreneurs. I suspect you'll be able to write a book about it someday and then get back on that speaking circuit. Until then, your goals and focus for xyz Inc seem clear. Reaching £12m/month of recurring revenue by 2025 with two-thirds of that coming from outside of the UK requires your team of Sales Managers to rapidly create effective sales

---

operations in their respective markets together with an overlay from your International Account Team that capitalises on the existing excellent relationships with the major European and US OEMs. The US, Germany and Iberia in particular have been selected as markets to 'bet on' and the current working plan is to hire x6 field-based, no-fly salespeople in each market who can deploy a regionally adapted version of your sales system and address the opportunity with the 18k dealers in the US, the 16k dealers in Germany and the 5k dealers in Iberia plus, of course, the OEMs in each market.

You'll remember the example of how we've helped ttfn Ltd to grow their sales outside of the UK to more than £100m and if you click here you can listen to the CEO explaining what we did for them.

I'm available on either 23rd or 3rd to talk further. Which would suit you best? Perhaps we bring Dick into the next conversation? Meantime, feel free to send me that NDA and I'll be glad to sign by return.

Best regards,

Notice the flattery? Too much? Well, maybe, but I really was enthused about what this guy had done and I saw no reason why I shouldn't show it. You'll be unsurprised to learn that he's a real extrovert and so naturally I wanted to appeal to his personality. For another personality type then of course I'd have toned it down a bit. Honest!

Notice the specificity? Numbers, places, job titles, industry jargon, it's all there. The second paragraph is 181 words. That's a synthesis of a 90-minute, x2-cup-of-tea conversation. It's not easy to do but with practice you'll get better and better and, when you come to writing a proposal for this, you're going to find this super helpful.

In fact, these emails are kind of like my own version of CRM. Having a record of all of these meetings safely tucked away in my sent items has saved my bacon on quite a few occasions. Doing so many C2Cs means that I naturally don't remember the content of all of them and oftentimes my notes look like they've been written by a three-year-old. By staying visible on platforms like LinkedIn, former C2C counterparties sometimes get back in touch many months later, and in a few cases many years after the meeting. Having the playback email enables me to quickly remember what we talked about and, with a quick bit of updated research, then have a more successful re-match.

Notice the link to a case study? We record video interviews with senior stakeholders of former clients who've achieved impressive outcomes. Guess what the structure of these 120-second films are. Dragon, Knight, Happily Ever After.

Notice the alternative dates, the suggestion of adding someone to the next meeting (he did and boy did that turn out to be important) and the NDA invitation (got done the same day and had me feeling pretty darn good about myself that evening!).

Not sure anyone ever acknowledged my coerced birthday party thank-you notes – actually, I recall them being the kind where you just filled in the blanks so it's not that surprising – but since I've grown up (kinda) I can't tell you the number of times that getting these notes right has delivered presents that might even rival my Raleigh Chopper bike when I was eight!

SUMMARY

If you've managed to read all of this chapter (well done by the way, I did bang on a bit there), then you'll get that we've really, really thought about these first meetings.

It's taken thousands upon thousands of C2Cs to decode them and determine what makes the difference. When you're an experienced businessperson who no doubt has done thousands of meetings yourself it can be tough to go back to school on what it takes.

We've had a number of new Positive Momentum consultants listen to this stuff a bit piously and explain how this isn't their first rodeo and that they know how to do a 'sales appointment' thank you very much. Off they trot and do (generally not enough) C2Cs, where they do most of the talking, telling the client where they are going wrong, why they are the answer to their problems and expecting to be hired there and then.

Never works out. Never will.

As Gary says, 'Be a good apprentice'.

☑ The relationship is all that matters.

☑ Prospective clients can smell fear.

☑ Don't be choosy about who you will and won't meet.

☑   Be a preparation obsessive.

☑   Prepare five questions for every meeting.

☑   Be imaginative about where you meet.

☑   Always send and carefully craft follow up messages.

Get free resources on making the most of meetings

The Positive Momentum Network will give you more tips and advice related to making the most of meetings, along with other resources, information and support for independent consultants. Sign up for free at **www.positivemomentum.com/network**

Part 4

Winning & Delivering Work

CHAPTER 7

Developing Relationships

Patience Pays

My first meeting with the client who has since connected me to more opportunities than any other started in typically unusual fashion. He'd just sold his data intelligence business to a very large company where I was engaged with coaching the management team (*my client there had been introduced to me by one of my seven founder clients from the restaurant picture in Chapter 2*).

Following the acquisition, this guy, who didn't know me from Adam, was staying on and was becoming part of that team, so I'd been asked to go and meet him to begin to involve him in the wider programme.

I'd been pre-briefed that he was plain speaking and didn't take prisoners, so I was prepared for a conversation that might very likely question the real value of my kind of work. Obviously, I'd done my homework – as I later learnt, I'd have been out on my ear if I hadn't – and though I think his expectations were pretty low, I came out of our first encounter unscathed and with his tentative endorsement of what I was doing, though 90% of the meeting was him answering my numerous questions about his business and perspectives.

Over the course of the next few years we did a little business together, nothing massive, but I plugged away gently at the relationship because... well, because it's what I do.

He eventually left the company that had bought his business and went to set up a new division of one of the world's largest media companies. Fantastic, I thought, but no, despite my overtures, no dice there. It wasn't until he was unexpectedly invited to become the CEO of a mid-sized media business in trouble (five years after we'd first met), that my fortunes changed – and changed enormously.

Before he started in the new role, we met at his golf club and had tea on the lawn one beautiful late summer's day in 2011. He hadn't been formally announced yet, but he had something he wanted to talk to me about and so he, I and his new HR Director sat down in convivial surroundings for the beginning of what would become an incredible 10 years (and counting) client, and now friend, relationship.

I'd led a couple of small sales conferences for him at the firm that had bought his, and he wanted to run a big sales conference for his new company very early the following year. (In fact, we ran one every year for the next five years and they became legendary events in the firm.)

Now, I love putting together and leading conferences. They're a huge amount of fun; I'm told I'm not bad at doing them and I really believe in their impact when well constructed. But the truth is that it's an isolated product. It's a nice annual deal but I was already doing so much more with other clients and was determined that he see me in a more expansive and strategic light.

Yet again, my pre-meeting research was the difference that made the difference.

Although this media company was privately owned (jointly by Private Equity and a large British newspaper group) they were in fact publishing their (not at all pretty) results and so I'd taken the time to go through them and prepare some questions. Long story short, what was due to be a quick meeting about a conference five months away turned into a much longer meeting about the myriad issues the organisation was facing with delivering top-line growth and a request for a proposal as to how I might be able to help with several key issues in the coming few months.

Since that meeting colleagues and I have been very privileged to play a part in the dramatic transformation of this now listed information, data and analytics company. We've travelled all over the world to work with their teams, been introduced through them to countless other clients and even benefit from this CEO's presence on our advisory board.

Throughout the early stages of our relationship there are countless ways I could have blown it:

► I could have allowed the fact that his company had been bought by my client, and that I was therefore somehow 'safe', to make me complacent about that first meeting.

► I could have pushed too hard for more business in the years between first meeting him and him being appointed CEO at the media firm.

► I could have stayed in my conference-guy box and allowed others to provide the services that I knew I was capable of.

I'd love to say that I knew that the golf club moment would come but of course I really didn't. I simply kept working this system. Investing in the relationship. Staying interested and visible. Being there for when the moment was right.

Just one of many chess games. But boy is this one paying off.

*I've long since
stopped worrying about
the label and instead
just love the work.*

MYTHBUSTERS

As I've said before, one of the things you're going to be repeatedly asked by well-meaning people who are only trying to help is, 'What's your proposition?' Remember how Sarah thought she needed one?

We're in a business world obsessed by propositions – and for most B2B organisations they really need to be. Competition is intense, true differentiation short lived at best and attention spans of buyers increasingly limited.

But you are not a commodity. There is only one of you. Your blend of experiences, personality, approach, contacts and opinions is utterly unique.

Now of course, you could try to come up with some cheesy description for what you do that attempts to differentiate – for a while I tried 'Motivational Engineer'. I know 😔, right?

Please don't. You're better than that.

Instead, just accept the blandness of 'consultant' and otherwise roll with what clients think you can do.

If you asked 10 of my clients 'What does Matt do?', you'd likely get 15 different answers, and some might not be very polite! I've been described as a consultant, a coach, a trainer, a speaker, a facilitator and probably loads of other odd things. Clients can call me an aardvark for all I care. I've long since stopped worrying about the label and instead just love the work.

I've clients who only use me for their executive team and wouldn't let me near the rest of their leaders. I've other clients to whom the door to the executive floor will always be closed for me, but I'm their go-to guy for leadership development. I've long since stopped worrying about the titles of the people I'm helping and instead just commit myself to them whoever they are.

I've clients who think I'm an expert in accelerating growth but shouldn't be allowed anywhere near change programmes and plenty who feel the exact opposite. I've long since stopped worrying about what the reason is for engaging and instead just feel immensely fortunate for the opportunities I do get.

Of course, I'm constantly trying to expand my network's sense of what I do. I publish regular articles on a range of topics where I feel I have expertise. I'm not shy about asking satisfied clients for written testimonials, even video case studies. And I'm none too subtle about name dropping into C2Cs the other client engagements I'm doing.

All of these things are intended to enable clients to hire me in the way that best suits them. I may not be especially cheap but I am incredibly easy to hire.

MINDSET

Don't get stuck in a box

Perhaps you want to be known for just one thing?

Nothing wrong with that in theory, but you'd better be truly outstanding at that thing otherwise you've some very hard yards ahead.

I was once compering a roadshow series of conferences for a client where they had hired a world renowned mountaineer with an incredible story to tell. To be honest, I'm rarely convinced of the value of speeches at corporate events from people outside of the world of business, but this guy was something else.

He told his story brilliantly, the images were magnificent and the links to the world of business were made crystal clear without being patronising. Every member of every audience loved him, and he was naturally referenced by every subsequent speaker for the rest of the day; for me that is always the acid test.

What I didn't understand was that he never took the opportunity to spend time with the clients. He'd turn up 30 minutes before his speech just to get mic'd up and then disappear immediately after what was normally a standing ovation.

Just before his final speech of the roadshow series I was sitting backstage with him and we were chatting while the audience was on a coffee break. I told him how great I thought his speech was and suggested that perhaps today after he'd finished I could introduce him to some of the leadership team for the client, as I was certain there was more he could do to help them in other ways.

He looked at me like I was a complete idiot. And trust me I know that look!

'Why on earth would I want to do that?' he rhetorically asked. 'An agency tells me where to be and when. I tell my story, I get paid, I go off and climb another mountain. I don't want to do anything else for this company.'

I got it.

It even made me think for a nanosecond or two that perhaps I should just focus on speaking, but then I remembered that I'm just a farmer's son from the Midlands with a bit of a career story and a big mouth, not an intrepid mountaineer who broke his leg falling off an ice cliff, got separated and left for dead by his partner and then spent three days dragging himself back to base camp through unbelievably treacherous terrain and weather!

I'm very proud of my expertise. I believe strongly in my business instincts. But the reality is that I'm just one of hundreds of thousands of people who claim to be able to help organisations do better.

Whilst clients might not be able to hire another Matt Crabtree (phew, huh?!), there are a remarkable number of similarly qualified people in the world and so if I'm to treat this as a business – and by now you know that I do – then I need a way of maximising my yield (remember, total billings in a year divided by the number of days you bill?) and for me that's about being supremely flexible in the way I engage with clients.

In any one week (indeed, sometimes in any one day) you'll find me working with people one-to-one, working with groups of anything from two to 2,000 or working entirely on my own developing new strategies for a particular client. You'll find me being the catalyst for clients to come up with their own solutions and you'll find me coming up with solutions at the behest of a client. You'll find me developing entirely new methodologies and you'll find me banging on about stuff I've been talking about for years.

(How many times do you think I've talked to people about BGQs?!)

In case it's not obvious, I've a low boredom threshold.

Not only do I love the diversity of clients and engagements that I'm lucky enough to work with, but it also provides me with the widest possible range of opportunities.

Perfect for soothing that ever-present paranoia.

TRAP TO AVOID
Resist the Pressure to Specialise

If you've a background anything like mine and want to enjoy the greatest possible range of opportunities then politely ignore those who implore you to become a 'specialist' in a 'niche'.

Resist the urge to spend days of your life trying to come up with the new alchemy of business (SPOILER ALERT: it doesn't exist) and then turning it into some amazing acronym.

Create a simple website if you want but don't get hauled in by some web developer who tells you they can somehow magically SEO the site so that you come top of Google when someone searches for a consultant. If you're going to make the effort to make yourself visible to people who know you (or who know people who know you) and if you're going to get out and meet lots of people doing C2Cs in the way I'm advocating, then please don't now go and blow it all by offering a range of cookie-cutter, off-the-shelf services.

You're not cloud software.

You can decide to engage in an infinite range of ways.

And above all else, it's an engagement we're after here.

The chance to prove your value in exchange for reward.

Who cares what it's called, how it's structured or even how much of it there is to begin with?

Let's not let ourselves be pigeon-holed. Let's get in under the radar. Let's give new clients what they want rather than what we think they need and then let's quietly develop the relationship to provide them with value, and ourselves with income, for the long term.

TOOLKIT

So, let's get back to that brilliant C2C you just had.

The one with the colleague from 10 years ago that you'd thought you'd lost touch with but who accepted your LinkedIn invitation to connect within an hour.

The one that surprised you when they responded positively to your brilliantly worded email invitation for a coffee at your (modest) club.

The one that you'd prepared thoroughly for and had some good (maybe even bloody good) questions in hand.

The one where halfway through they said 'Now, that's a good question' and you told a quick killer story of a time when you'd helped solve just such a dilemma in the past.

And the one that you followed up with the perfect email, playing back their situation, suggesting you sign an NDA (which they sent straightaway) and booking a time to get together with some more people from their side.

I'm not saying these happen every day, but an effective approach to every step along this process increases the probability of the next to the extent that you'll probably be getting one of these per week within a few short months.

In other words, that's more real opportunities than you could possibly fulfi l if they all came to fruition.

And the reality is that they won't.

As we push forward toward the denouement of our operating system, we now enter the zone of an increasing number of variables that are outside of your control.

At any one time I've between five and ten pretty good looking new opportunities on top of my existing engagements. Situations where the person/people I'm speaking with say that they really want to work with me. Situations where we've agreed what, how and sometimes even when the work will be happening. Some will have even received a proposal (more on getting them right soon) that has been 'signed off' according to my sources.

And then you get the Dear John email. The 'it's not you, it's us' note, full of apologies and often promising this isn't 'no, never' it's 'just not now'.

The ones where a new boss arrives and puts stuff like this on hold.

The ones where the organisation is suddenly being bought by someone else and the organisational deck is being reshuffled.

The ones where the strategy changes and this issue becomes less relevant.

The ones where the dog ate their homework…

1. Dealing with rejection

To this day these rejection notes still sting. Petulant irritation with the potential client quickly gives way to self-criticism as I reflect on what I could have done better. Sometimes I convince myself that it was more of a thing than it really was and sometimes that I should go back and 'handle the objection' as we used to teach in the 1980s. Then I look at my whiteboard and see the other live opportunities and remind myself for the thousandth time that this is an unpredictable numbers game and that, as long as I keep throwing logs on the fire, all will be well.

So I *don't* try some smarmy and unbecoming objection-handle email but instead I send an empathetic reply.

I then leave them for a few weeks, sometimes a few months. Then I go all the way back to the start and send them a carefully worded email to invite them to a C2C to hear how things are going for them. With patience and determination, sometimes over years, they can end up being a meeting in the rare English sunshine next to the clubhouse of a golf course...

But, what the hell to do in the meantime?

Well, you've heard all my rhetoric about getting out and opening some new lines of enquiry, so I don't suppose you want to hear that again...

So instead, let me offer you some of our favourite chess game plays. Set pieces that, when the conditions are right and they're played at the right moment, can have a miraculous effect on your fortunes.

Send them a book or an article

Another thing that causes my accountant consternation is the £1,000 or so that I spend on books for clients every year. In fact, even Amazon gets a bit confused as it regularly warns me about buying the same book for the umpteenth time. (*Top one currently is* The First 90 Days *by Michael Watkins, purchased 14 times in the last year apparently!*)

The world is drowning in information – some of it useful, most of it not – and our potential clients have never been more time poor. Enter the well-read consultant who, following an interesting C2C, is able to send a book that might just hit the spot for the situation in which the client finds themselves.

Now I know people who would never send a book to a client unless it was their own. They ask, 'Why risk losing an opportunity by giving the client the answer from someone else?'

Well, if it were possible for every client to solve every issue they faced by reading a book, then I don't think consulting would exist as an industry. Have an abundant state of mind to stuff like this. Be what Ken Blanchard in *Gung Ho!* called 'a big pie person'.

My repeated experience is that this pays you back more than often enough. It's so easy to jump on Amazon and send a book to someone with a short gift note.

On one occasion that I did this, the client then hired the (rather famous at the time) author of the book I'd sent him to speak at a leadership event they were running. I'll admit I was a bit irked when he first told me, until a few days later when the client not only invited me to attend but also to host the event, for which I was handsomely paid. The client then publicly (and very kindly) in front of their top

100 leaders credited me with having brought this thought leader to their attention. This happened just before the author's speech so I did have a few moments of worry that he might be awful! Fortunately, he was amazing.

Of course, plenty of people have neither the time nor the inclination to read a book on a specific business topic. Equally, there often isn't a book that quite covers the specificity of an issue a client is facing.

But I bet there's an article out there that does.

The big beasts in the consulting industry have almost become publishers in their own right. The quality of their insights and their investment in producing a constant stream of freely accessible content is utterly remarkable and improving all the time.

They know that only one in every 1,000 people who read their articles hires them and they don't care. They know that they're helping to make the business world a better place – and that of course the one client is worth multiple millions and pays for this service many times over.

As well as the consulting industry, business media outlets like *HBR, Fortune, Forbes, Business Week, The FT, The Wall Street Journal, Fast Company, Inc, Visual Capitalist, The Economist* etc, etc, are putting out material on a near hourly basis that is increasingly engaging and on point.

You name a business issue, however narrow, and I guarantee you'll find a recent article out there offering free, topical advice written brilliantly.

With articles, I get a bit old school, though I prom-ise there's method in my admittedly less than completely environmentally responsible madness. When I find an arti-cle online or in a magazine that I think a potential/existing client might like, I print it out, I stick a Post-It note on it saying 'saw this and thought of you, love Matt' (well, maybe not the love bit, but you get the idea), fold it up, put it in an envelope and mail it to them...

Now I know there are copyright issues here. I'm care-ful to respect that by making sure I pay for downloadable PDFs where they exist, and I certainly never try to imply that this material is my own. The printouts always include the author's details and their copyrights. I'm certain I'm still infringing something with this approach but I'm hoping that since it's hardly the crime of the century the authorities will go easy on me upon reading this guilty plea.

'Why not just send a web link, you luddite?' I hear you cry.

Well, how many emails do you get on a daily basis versus how many people send you a piece of paper in the post?

I'm not ashamed of the fact that I want to be remembered, and the best way I know how to do that is to be different.

Around 75% of the people to whom I send printed articles, and 99% of people I send books, respond in some fashion. I don't think that would be anything like as high – and it would definitely be forgotten much more quickly – if I was only sending web links by email.

You'll perhaps remember the story of the *A Brit's Guide to Orlando* book from Chapter 2? I'd estimate that

that single action has triggered somewhere in the region of £5m in consulting income so far and I can track wins just in recent weeks back to that small investment.

Offer to run a survey

Often our engagements include an online survey as part of the pre- or post- programme formalities, but we'll some-times offer to run one for a potential client as a demon-stration of good will and commitment.

Thanks to the predominance of platforms like Survey Monkey and countless others, it's incredibly quick and easy to set up a short survey and have the client share the link with a community of respondents to whom you can assure anonymity and independence of data analysis.

Some quick tips on setting up these kind of pre-en-gagement surveys:

▶ Take care with collecting information that identifies the respondent in any way. For a start, it causes alarm bells to ring for the respondent but more importantly you'll have data protection obligations that can be both complex and onerous, though of course you should anyway be registered with the relevant authorities in your jurisdiction for holding client information, even if it's only a few invoices.

▶ Take care not to ask too many questions. If your survey takes any more than 2–3 minutes to complete then you'll likely end up with a very poor response rate.

► Take care to ask one thing per question. If you ask 'How open and engaging do you consider your manager?' I won't know whether to answer about 'open' or 'engaging'.

► Take care not to get too distracted by the dizzying options on offer from your preferred platform supplier. A simple Likert scale statement (typically five choices between Totally and Not at all) is usually just fine rather than a drag and drop ranking list or other fancy-pants options.

► Take care your survey statements don't seem like they're leading the respondent to dis their organisation or colleagues. Of course you're looking for an angle but be neutral, even positive in statement construction. For example, 'How effective would you say your organisation is at recycling?' is much better than 'How wasteful do you consider your organisation to be?'

► Finally, take care to consider the report you want to share with the client after the survey is closed. What is the hypothesis you are seeking to prove and what is your potential client (or their stakeholders) most interested in? As with many things in life, start with the end in mind.

Buy some shares

I have a few hundred (in some cases a few thousand) pounds worth of shares in all my clients who are publicly listed.

I always invest before they hire me. It's become almost a superstition that if I don't, they won't hire me!

Many have actually been a fantastic investment, but that's not why I do it.

I want to put my money where my mouth is. I want to show potential clients that I believe in their potential – and of course, I'm not shy about telling them that I've done that.

Now, of course there are laws that restrict anyone with, what the SEC for example calls 'possession of material, nonpublic information' from trading shares in a particular company and so, on the odd occasions that our engagements provide access to that kind of secret squirrel stuff, I'm ultra-careful not to buy – or sell.

However, the reality is that we're rarely exposed to such sensitive information and by having the stock ticker on your investment app with some of your own money behind it, you'll have another reason to keep them in mind and maybe notice an event that creates a legitimate excuse for contact.

Become a customer

For anything we buy as a company, we've always first sought out a company that's either already a client or one where we know people and where there is, therefore, a chance they might become a client. Our banks, our lawyers, our accountants, our IT providers are all either clients or are quietly being propagated as such.

Of course this move is easier with a consumer products company.

For a while we worked with an investment company that owned several fashion brands, one of which made mid-priced men's suits. I took the opportunity to purchase one of their suits and at an event they were running met the Group CEO for the first time – my contacts were a level below him. Ever-observant, before we'd even shaken hands he noticed that the suit was one of theirs. I'm not saying I won more work because I wore one of their suits, but it was another little pebble in the pond.

Bring them a customer

Even if you can't become a customer, what about other businesses you know that you could introduce? Every organisation is always interested in a new client, and I've lost count of the number of clients who now trade with each other because of an introduction we've made.

We never ask for or accept introductory fees and are careful not to be seen as a formal intermediary. Our independence is too important to us.

If we think there's an opportunity – and we're looking for these a lot as this is a master chess move – we'll start by asking the party that we think could become a customer if they'd mind if we introduced them. Assuming we get the green light – full disclosure: in around a third of cases we don't – then we'll make the introduction to the most senior person we can and then step away.

Help them fill a vacancy

The challenge of finding great people to fill key roles is a very common C2C subject and, whilst I'm not trying to take away business from our cousins in the recruitment industry, as I suggested before if you can introduce a good candidate from your network then that's a real high value chess move.

Now of course, the danger here is that an existing client will be peeved to say the least if you recommend one of their talented people to another client. Don't kid yourself that they won't find out it was you.

I've always operated on the basis that existing clients are off limits for this activity.

However, the sun rises and sets on every client relationship and whilst I'm always plotting ways to get back into the arms of those who loved us previously, after a couple of years, I don't feel it's unreasonable to make the odd introduction.

Again, we never ask for or accept fees for these introductions, preferring the long (and in my view much more lucrative) game of having a sponsor on the inside. As your network grows it can be hard to remember everyone you're connected to, but a quick search of your first level connections in LinkedIn of the title that someone is seeking candidates for can trigger your memory and create an opportunity.

Help them expand their network

It might not be that they need a new employee, but who doesn't welcome a new professional contact? Senior leadership roles are often pretty lonely places and being able to compare notes with someone doing a similar role in perhaps a completely different industry can be refreshing and excellent.

Oftentimes, it's simply been because one person I know reminds me of another, or the issues that someone is facing are remarkably similar to those that I know someone else has just faced. I don't overthink these introductions. Sometimes they go somewhere, sometimes they don't. I'm pretty sure no one has ever been offended by my efforts in this respect.

2. LinkedIn newsfeed activity

Yes, I know, LinkedIn again 🥱 but it really is rocket fuel for developing your practice if you use it well.

In Chapter 5 we talked about how to engage in your newsfeed but now I'm going to attribute a nominal value to the various pings you can send out to your network via this platform.

LinkedIn features from 2022, so if you're reading this in the future you can both laugh at these rudimentary features and create your own version of the below.

(I'll use GBP as my base currency; I'm sure you get the idea.)

▶ **Like = 5p**

It's nice to give someone a thumbs up (other emojis are available) for a post and it's something you ought to be doing every day, if not multiple times per day, but in terms of pebbles in the pond it's a bit like a grain of sand.

▶ **Comment = 10p – 30p**

Much better is to make a comment but only if it's got some substance. So many people just drop the 'Congrats, great news' type blurb which adds little to anyone. Far better is to say something that builds on the content of the post and/or reminds the person who posted it of your existence more substantially. If it's a link to an article, I'll often reference a specific passage of that. If it's a good news story from a client, I'll often shamelessly hint at our involvement.

▶ **Share = ?**

It's widely known that, at time of writing, shares don't feature very prominently in the author's feed (they get a quick notification but nothing else) and are well known for getting very low reaction rates.

Many believe this feature will soon be retired. Personally, I prefer a well-worded Comment than a Share.

▶ **Native post of someone else's content = 50p**

Now that you're doing all this reading, LinkedIn offers a fabulous place to post great content you've found elsewhere. Include a short comment from you on why it's so great and otherwise let someone else do the talking. The most highly rated and commented upon post I've ever done was a simple share of an excellent HBR article called 5 *Things Highly Performing Teams Do Differently.* The same day I posted it, a former client got in touch about some work with their team. A coincidence?

At the time of writing LinkedIn offers you two ways to post your own content:

▶ **Native post of your own content = 0p – 100p**

A post can contain up to 3,000 characters as well as photos, videos, documents and even polls, though why the world might need any more of them is frankly a mystery to me.

Numerous hashtags, web links and @ call-outs of people/organisations are of course all de rigueur for these to maximise the look-at-me-ness.

I've given these kinds of posts a very wide range of implied value because so many are just vacuous, nauseating, virtue signalling, and even downright narcissistic. PT Barnum said there is no such thing as bad publicity but looking at some people's posts I'm really not so sure...

If you've got something to say that you think will make the business world a better place then brilliant, please post about it.

If you need some help with something then let us all know and we'll do all we can, please post about it.

If you want to commend a person or an organisation on good work they've done, then there are few better places, please post about it.

But if you've just got a new car or want to have a rant about something or have just given some money to a deserving cause, please find another outlet...

▶ **Native article of your own content = 0p – 150p**

The other option is LinkedIn's own blog platform. At time of writing you get to that by clicking 'Write Article'.

You'll see that I give this the highest potential implied value but for the same reasons as described above these can also be total bilge.

An article can contain up to 100k characters, though clearly anyone using all of those up better have something of absolutely earth shattering importance to say!

The virtue of writing articles is that the 'views' you get mean much, much more than a post since they represent someone consciously clicking your title.

(For a Post the 'views' number simply represents how many times someone saw it in their newsfeed, typically for nanoseconds.)

PRO TIP
Writing Articles

▶ *Write at least one article per month, ideally one per fortnight.*

▶ *Don't overthink the content.*

▶ *Start writing lots of articles in the 'My Drafts' section of LinkedIn articles under the 'Publishing Menu'.*

▶ *Use discussions with clients or current affairs as inspiration for articles.*

▶ *Write only about topics you have known expertise in.*

1. *Consider a topical business challenge on which you have a fresh perspective.*

2. *Develop three actionable and distinctive ideas to resolve the challenge.*

3. *Recall an anecdote relevant to this topic.*

4. *Write a really compelling opening sentence.*

5. *Develop an opening paragraph or two that hooks the reader.*

6. *Write a paragraph for each idea.*

7. *Write a final paragraph that bookends the opening paragraph.*

8. *Write a simple, clickable headline 'how to, three ways to, the secret to' etc.*

9. *Select a banner image and an image for each idea.*

10. *Have someone proofread the article.*

11. *Publish early Tue/Thu morning on LinkedIn, Twitter and Facebook with at least three #s.*

▶ *Observe who engages.*

▶ *Respond to all comments.*

▶ *Test and Learn.*

3. 'Remember' stuff

In the nearly 20 years that I've been an independent consultant there have been thousands upon thousands of both personal and professional life events with my network that I've been exposed to.

Since I like people (and I hope that you do too as nothing in this book will resolve that issue), I'm naturally interested to learn about their lives to the extent that they want to share. For example, my kids have grown from babies to accomplished young women during the time that I've been consulting and so naturally they come up in conversation with clients who also have offspring. I've had numerous casual conversations lamenting the challenges of sleepless nights, school choices, even boyfriends, as the border between professional and personal relationships is inevitably often blurred. I've even had some of my clients' teenage children come and work shadow me – though goodness only knows what that taught them!?

Now my memory for names, places and events that come up in less formal conversations isn't the best and I hate it when I see someone again six months later, know with certainty that they told me about a dream holiday they were due to be taking, but I can't remember for the life of me where they went.

PRO TIP
Use Your Phone Notes

So here's what I do straight after meetings where I learn something new in this zone. Please don't judge me too harshly...

In my Contacts app on my phone, I use the Notes section to record the names of children, spouses, bosses, football teams, holiday home destinations, major upcoming life events etc, etc.

Then, just before I see them next, I open up the app and check the details.

Does it make me sound superficial? Well maybe, but personally I'd far rather ask how Johnny and Emma are doing than say, 'So, how are the kids?' and hope that they did have more than one – or indeed any at all!

Our lives are full of key moments and events and, whilst social media increasingly makes many of these easy to acknowledge in a one-click perfunctory manner, there is still plenty that happens beyond the digital-push realm that by 'remembering' you can make a positive impression on someone.

On the professional side, key upcoming meetings are a fantastic opportunity for a quick encouraging text message. I've countless reminders in my diary for dates when I know a contact has a board presentation or is giving a speech at an industry event. A short message that morning is more than just a nice thing to do, it's another pebble in the pond.

We often even send gifts for key milestones.

My golf club meeting client from the start of this chapter recently hit the 10 year mark in his role. We produced a framed, one-metre long image that marked all of the acquisitions, divestments and key milestones over that decade and presented it to him. We were amazed (and a bit smug) to later discover that it now has pride of place on their boardroom wall.

Of course a nice bottle of something, some flowers or just a book works well too!

4. Get an NDA signed

You've already heard me advocate for suggesting you ask potential clients if you can sign one of these, but why are they so effective in moving the game forward?

Well, an NDA is a relatively formal exercise in most organisations. They generally need to be requested, perhaps from a colleague in a legal department, and then someone with the authority to do so needs to countersign it. That might not be the person we're dealing with. In fact, it might be someone we never actually meet but who has overall say over whether we get in the door or not.

A signed NDA from the client is a fantastic indication that they're serious about working with you. If they don't want you to sign one, then either that's just not their jam or maybe this opportunity isn't such a real thing after all.

As I explained earlier, I never read and therefore never challenge the content of clients' NDAs. I know that I probably should, but I don't have the time or the interest and, in any event, I can't believe that the kind of reputable organisations we work with would have me sign something that wasn't above board. Of course, I might have signed away my house several times but honestly I don't think so...

If you have a law degree you'll think I'm a fool at this point – I warn you, it's going to get worse later when we talk about contracts – but for now, just focus on being easy to work with, especially in these crucial pre-engagement moments.

SUMMARY

The journey from contact to contract is never the same. There are some factors you can control but many you can't, and too many people give up at the first hurdles.

They're too dependent on too few opportunities, they don't have an abundant outlook and are not generous with their time, interest and resources. Don't be like them. Be a Grand Master of Consulting Chess - and a jolly good person to boot.

Get free resources on developing relationships

The Positive Momentum Network will give you more tips and advice related to developing relationships, along with other resources, information and support for independent consultants. Sign up for free at **www.positivemomentum.com/network**

CHAPTER 8

Sealing the Deal

A Decent Proposal

My favourite win of recent years was when I was selected for an engagement by a former McKinsey consultant.

You'll have seen me reference McKs on various occasions throughout this book and, in my view, at the present time they are the gold standard of our industry. I'm not saying they are perfect by any means, and I consider their general lack of consultants with real world experience to be a real gap – but it's a gap I'm happy is there so that you and I can fill it in our own small ways.

When a colleague told me (just a month before the pandemic) about a guy he knows who had just got a job as the CEO of the EV charging division of a major energy company and was potentially looking for some help with his executive team, I was excited to meet with him. As an early adopter of electric cars, it's an industry I'm really interested in but hadn't got anywhere near before.

Then he told me that he used to be a McKinsey consultant.

Now, no disrespect to former McKers, but on previous occasions that I've met them they have rather looked down on me and my firm and I'd certainly never been hired by one. I suspect they train their consultants to have a somewhat superior attitude and so, to be honest, I didn't go into this meeting with high hopes.

Of course, I did all the usual preparation that you've heard about a hundred times by now, and on arrival made full use of the complimentary ultra-fast charging station at their office, but I didn't really think I'd be going back again.

Upon meeting the CEO I wasn't remotely surprised by his intellect. He'd only been there for a few short weeks but had already completed a detailed assessment of the situation and developed a compelling transformation strategy for the future.

What did surprise me, however, was how welcoming he was of someone from a relatively (in fact, to him completely) unknown firm. He had none of the arrogance my prejudice had me expecting and instead treated me like an equal from the get-go. Of course, having been introduced by someone he knew and trusted was a massive advantage and it's why our system is focused – as you know only too well by now – on doing business with people you know, or who know people you know.

Following this surprisingly good first meeting, he asked me to prepare a proposal.

And then COVID arrived…

Whilst the pandemic did much less damage to my business than I might have feared – in fact, we actually grew, to take nothing away from the pain and suffering it has caused countless families all around the world – it did, however, make very early stage conversations like this quite challenging.

We kept talking – on video by now, of course – and naturally there was delay after delay as every time we thought we might have a way forward we were thwarted by another health restriction that limited the way we could engage.

As it turned out, these delays actually worked hugely in my favour since, every time we spoke, this potential client would suggest another improvement to the as yet unapproved proposal document. Whilst I might childishly imagine that McKinsey train their consultants to be superior (pot, kettle anyone?), I know for certain that they train them to within an inch of their life to produce outstanding client documents, so I knew the bar would be high.

I thought my first attempt was pretty good but by version four my potential client had inadvertently given me a masterclass in how to take something (to coin a phrase) From Good to Great.

He helped me to upgrade it so that the current context was better synthesised, the value was much more clearly articulated and he showed me how to build more modularity and optionality, both in terms of the solution as well as the pricing.

Why would someone with the title CEO bother with all this document to-ing and fro-ing? Couldn't he just make the decision on the strength of having met me?

Well, you see he wasn't able to make this decision without approval from the mothership. He had to show it to people that I didn't know, would never meet and would have even less clue about who I was than he did.

The parent company is VERY big. They have strict procurement policies, preferred supplier lists, even their own in-house consultants. If I hadn't already encountered (and overcome) these things many times before I might have been put off.

He needed a document that would blow any concerns they might have about dealing with an unknown out of the water. And thanks to him, and his vigorous red pen, it worked.

Despite the restrictions of the pandemic, we got started with virtual sessions in the autumn of 2020 and, once lockdown had passed, even managed to get the team together physically for an in-person event. We had 10 of us in a room big enough for 50, with all the windows open and enough sanitiser to bathe in.

MYTHBUSTERS

You can never predict the final stages before you're finally appointed.

I've sold to some of the world's largest organisations and it's been unbelievably easy, and I've sold to some tiny organisations that make an unbelievable meal of the process. And of course vice versa.

I've signed 150+ page contracts (that I honestly haven't read a word of) and I've had clients ask me to work through other intermediaries as contracting directly would take so long that by the time it was done we'd all be retired.

I've been paid upfront in cash (that was an odd one) and I've waited more than 180 days for payment. (Never had a penny of bad debt, though.)

Clients are naturally, necessarily even, cautious, especially if they are dealing with a brand/person they've never come across directly before. Some organisations have had horrible prior experiences with consultants and the arrival of a new name can trigger all sorts of warning signals.

Getting the proposal right (in whatever format) for people you're never going to meet is always an effort worth going to. Especially with those very-nearly-now clients who tell you, 'Oh, just knock something rough together, it's really only a formality'. Hmm, I'm not falling for that one. At least, not again...

Engaging with an organisation's various purseholders positively, respectfully and with maximum flexibility is also a must. If you're the kind of person who likes to call the shots and dictate terms then you're going to find yourself spending a lot of time having pointless debates about minutiae that you'll never win.

If you want to fish where the big fish are (in fact, increasingly where any fish at all are) then often you're going to have to suck up some insulting payment terms, draconian contracts, irrational copyright demands, demanding SLAs and hideously slow processes with multiple parties in the same client who rarely talk to, or sometimes even claim to know, each other. Sounds joyful, huh?

It's not that bad. It's mostly down to you and how pragmatic you decide to be. And it's why I believe in the widest diversity of client base I can build.

Once you've built a steady stream of income from various clients, then (I very much hope) you'll give much less of a damn about all this stuff.

MINDSET

1. The proposal

Before we get into exactly how to make your best bended-knee proposal, let's explore when and what you should propose and how much for.

One of the ways to guarantee you waste a big chunk of your precious time (otherwise known as inventory) is to write speculative proposals.

At the end of a really great C2C it's so tempting to ask the client if they would like you to put together a proposal. It's rare that they say no. People either don't want to rain on your parade and/or they'd love to read your proposal in the event that they might one day buy from you. It's a bit like taking a brochure from the Ferrari garage. They look beautiful and why not; you never know, right?

We convince ourselves that we're leaping the chess game forward and toil for hours on our masterpiece only to find that they just weren't quite cooked yet. Worse than that, we can find that our contact at the client blunders into their boss with a proposal that's really not as well articulated as it would have been had there been another couple of conversations. It's the equivalent of blowing too hard on the embers of a fire...

Make the client ask you for a proposal. Ask them *'What's the next best step here?'* If you must suggest something, then make it an NDA or a follow-up meeting.

Just don't be the first party to say the word 'proposal'.

I've had a few occasions where I've never had to write a proposal at all. The answer to 'What's the next best step here?' was 'We get started and you send us an invoice'. It doesn't happen often but there's no chance of it if you suggest a proposal.

Independent consultants are often looking for the big win. That individual contract that's worth so much that they don't have to worry about all this stationery purchasing, coffee drinking, book buying, LinkedIn liking nonsense for a few months, maybe even a few years if they get lucky. The big spin of the wheel.

Whilst I've never landed one of these really big whales (not my bag), I've several Positive Momentum colleagues who have, and they do very well from them. Where they are solo engagements, they are generally pseudo-interim type arrangements and, if the price is right, my colleague is happy and, if we're preparing for the (sometimes unpredictable) end of the contract with some other potential client conversations, then great.

Of course, these types of engagement also come with an enormous health warning.

You can very easily get sucked into the day-to-day workings of the client to the extent that it's very difficult to determine the difference between this engagement and doing a full-time job for them. Except, of course, you've none of the benefits of being full-time…

Worse than that, you can become so busy with this one engagement that you've virtually no time for building a diverse practice and so you fall off a cliff edge when the contract finishes.

Gary's first contract was a four-day-per-week thing. The client really wanted him five days per week, but even then he was wise enough to fight for his Friday C2C days, which were normally packed with four to five meetings. My phone was generally red hot with Gary calls on Fridays! He soon built a multi-client practice and to this day enjoys a healthy combination of both large client commitments and smaller in-fill engagements.

In any event, tax authorities in many jurisdictions are increasingly clamping down on these types of engagements, making them harder to come by. However, they can still be great and are very much worth being open to when/if they arise.

My practice is amongst the most diverse in Positive Momentum. I'm generally working with between 15 and 20 clients who are each worth between £10k and £100k in annual billings.

I think it's a gap in the market that the big consulting firms don't want and where former leaders can provide outstanding input at a relative market premium. It's pretty much why we exist as Positive Momentum.

In years gone by I've had client concentration; in one year one client was worth 75% of my billings, and I really didn't like it.

That's not to say I'm a client commitment-phobe. Half of my currently active clients I've worked with for more than 10 years. With several of my key contacts I'm with them at their fifth or even sixth organisation since we first worked together.

It just seems that I took that 'We love having you around, just in short doses' comment from my last full-time corporate boss very much to heart.

This is where lots of the strands of our system start to come together.

A diverse practice means that I'm always learning and stimulated.

A diverse practice means that I don't need to over-push clients for deals.

And a diverse practice means that I'm financially secure.

It creates the confidence to charge a premium rate for my work.

So, let's finally explore the grubby question of how to tell people how much they need to invest to get your help.

TRAP TO AVOID
'What's your day rate?'

An innocent enough question, it seems, but it's another one we've become adept at evading.

Contractors work on day rates, not consultants.

Of course, whilst there is an overlap between contractors and consultants (see the high paying pseudo interim contracts referred to previously), our system is all about you winning a diverse practice of outcome-oriented, premium work that gives you freedom, fulfillment and security. It's not a system for day rate freelance contractors who generally only work with one client at a time.

Whilst every engagement you do ultimately comes back to how long you will have to spend doing it, when I propose an engagement, it's the deliverables and the outcomes, not the days spent toiling, that take centre stage.

2. Use their language

From the very first C2C with someone I've never met before I'm thinking about what a proposal might ultimately look like, should that path become open. I'm looking for the macro, and ideally measurable, goals that the organisation, function, team or individual has.

I'm writing down their exact patterns of language, their KPIs, their jargon so that if and when I get the chance to make a proposal, it's all going to be in their speak. I concentrate on this even more intensively on the occasions that I'm fortunate enough to work with clients from different cultures. Though I am ashamed to say that I speak no other language than English, I am an avid student of how different nationalities describe and react to things and work hard to always adapt to them rather than expecting them to adapt to me. This is all about establishing value and respectful rapport. The more familiar the language, the more likely that those involved in considering the investment will put pen to paper.

3. The CFO test

Too many consultants convey their proposed value in weak and weedy terms.

They worry about 'over-promising' and so end up with jargony, weasel-wordy waffle like 'optimise', 'maximise', 'leverage' or worst of all, 'synergise'. ☹

If you don't know the hard measures that your client's CFO is really interested in, then I'd suggest you're not ready to submit a convincing proposal.

If you're not confident enough to believe that whatever it is that you do, does in fact contribute, however indirectly, to the achievement of the organisation's macro goals, then you've chosen the wrong profession.

One of my favourite B2B billboard campaigns was from a 2012–15 series from Accenture (that reputedly had to be rushed out as a result of needing to remove a certain badly behaved golfer from their ads at short notice) and that features a real client in each ad. If you travelled much by air around that time, you'll have seen them above the security lines and baggage carousels. Taglines like 'We helped Marriot reach $7bn in annual sales online', 'We're helping UNIQLO grow by 350%' and '€1bn in savings for Unilever' were bold, client endorsed and achieved some of the best results of any campaign they'd ever run[2]. They're not trying to say they achieved these things single handedly, but the client was willing to credit the value they added – and it's the same kind of value that the likes of you and I add. We might not add (or save) billions but I'm certain that what I do over time helps to create millions in value, and, whilst

2 https://stevieawards.com/women/accentures-marketing-campaign

I'm reassuringly expensive, I don't (yet) charge millions in return.

'But I'm not selling to the CFO,' I hear you cry. *'My contact is in another function and several layers beneath the CFO.'*

And your point is??

If I'm going to go to the trouble of putting together a persuasive proposal, then I want to be damn sure that whoever's inbox it ends up in, they'll be rapidly convinced. You have no idea where your proposal will end up. Don't take the risk.

I win around two in three of the proposals I submit and that's because I don't submit that many, and the ones I do send get brutally scrutinised.

4. Be easy to buy from

Let me start this section by repeating something I briefly mentioned earlier and that's that I've never had a single penny of bad debt. Not only have none of my direct clients ever failed to pay but neither have any of my Positive Momentum colleagues' clients.

To date that's around $50m of revenues.

I realise that by putting this in writing I'm probably jinxing this fact, but I honestly don't see it changing. This hasn't happened because we've strict contracts and fierce credit controllers. If anything, we've a much more laissez-faire attitude to this stuff than most companies like us.

I really don't mind (and never have) whether a client wants to pay me stage by stage, all upfront or all at the end. I'm not going to get bent out of shape about their payment terms or their procurement policies. And I'm certainly not funny about somehow protecting our content against the very unlikely event that they decide to copy it. And even if they do, what is it they say about imitation?

We have no standard terms and conditions, other than preferring to be paid at 30 days but rarely bothering to even start chasing until around 60.

We pay all of our suppliers well before their payment terms because we think that's a responsible way to operate, especially since we tend to prefer to buy from smaller organisations where we're supporting up and coming entrepreneurs, particularly those with a social and/or environmental purpose.

If our clients choose to sit on their debt to us for longer... well, I don't like it but here's the thing – it's never got anything to do with our contacts. They're always mortified by their employers' poor payment behaviours and, because I don't want them to associate conversations with me with discomfort, I go easy on them.

To a point.

On the odd occasion – and I can count these on one hand – where a client has tried to wriggle out of paying, I've had no hesitation to use the full recourse of the law to retrieve what we are owed. I've succeeded both in my home country and elsewhere in the world. Push me or my colleagues too far on this and I'll take all legal means to ensure we get paid.

It might surprise you to learn that you don't need a written contract to have a binding, legally enforceable contract with your clients. Modern contract law in most countries accepts email communication where it's clear that the client was engaging your services – like approving a proposal or sending a purchase order number. I'm not saying having a contract wouldn't be better. I'm simply saying that the friction it adds to the process is completely disproportionate with the likely need to employ it.

Here's the funny thing: this extent of problem has never arisen where the client was a big organisation. Whilst some of them have truly terrible payment terms, they always pay in the end. Sad to say, but the only times it's been tricky have been with smaller, owner-managed businesses. For that reason we are often just a little more 'on it' with newer, smaller clients, when they go over the payment terms, sometimes asking for the first phase up-front, but even with them we're not Rottweilers.

When a client says yes, the next step for us is to send the first invoice with a Purchase Order number if they do that kind of thing, but certainly not some awful contract of ours. If they want us to sign *their* contract then no probs, ping it over and we'll sign it by return.

In fact, clients who send contracts to us are often astonished at how quickly we send the signed version back. 'Don't you want to get it checked by your legal department (☺)?' they ask. When I'm feeling mischievous, I often reply to this question by asking hypothetically if we had any issues with any of the contract terms whether *their* legal department would be agreeable to amendments? The reply to this is always somewhere between 'certainly not' and 'well, they might, but it will likely take a good few months'. QED.

5. Price it in phases

Our 'investment schedule' page (our pompous name for the bit where we tell the client how much) is nearly always broken up into phases. You'd commonly see sections titled with words like Discovery, Design or Delivery – unless, of course, the client described it in a different way. In which case, you'd see their language.

Depending on the scale or nature of the project, often the delivery/implementation phase itself is split into a series of sub phases. Rather than ask the client to commit to every phase up front, we're perfectly happy with a pay-as-you-go, keep-us-on-our toes approach.

Some clients really like this, some couldn't care less, but the one thing that's sure is that it's a real differentiator. Why most businesses like ours get their knickers in a twist over getting full commitment from their clients is beyond me, but as long as they do it's yet another handy little way for the likes of you and me to stand out from the crowd.

Remember, this is all making it easy for the client to get started with you. A small initial commitment might very well come under certain sign off thresholds and get you in 'under the radar'. Be confident that the value you create, even in the early phases, will be more than enough to give them the confidence they need to keep issuing those Purchase Orders. Your probability of success if you propose four stages of $7,750 is exponentially larger than if you propose one package of $25,000.

6. Outcome/risk-based pricing

Occasionally potential clients come up with the clever idea of suggesting that they either partially or even fully remunerate us based on whether our work actually delivers as intended.

I get asked whether I'll work this way around a couple of times per year, but it's never actually happened in the end. I suspect they've been put off by my position that if we're going to engage in that way then there will need to be some considerable upside to counterbalance our risk on the downside.

I'm not in principle against the idea of risking some/all of my fee, since I'm very happy to stand by the value that my efforts create, but I'll be expecting at least twice as much as I would if the client paid in the normal way.

I'll also be expecting a high level of transparency over what actually gets executed. If you want to reward me based on whether my advice delivers value then I (not unreasonably, I hope you agree) expect you to deploy my ideas in full.

With these conditions understood, every client who's ever suggested this way of working has ended up happily paying me in the normal way...

7. Volume discounting

Whilst our system advocates going in under the radar, the reality is that our effectiveness/staying power does often mean that our work with the client expands to the point where we appear on Procurement Traffic Control radar screens.

A few years ago I got the dreaded procurement team email from a very large global client who I was doing increasing numbers of engagements with at the time.

It was actually a very civil communication explaining that they'd like to take us through the process to become a Preferred Supplier, since they'd noticed we were being requisitioned so often.

All good and something we've done plenty of times before, but this time there was an interesting quirk.

The procurement team proposed to guarantee me a certain number of consulting days for the forthcoming year but in doing so would expect a discount to their usual rate.

Now here's a good dilemma – and a really good test of the strength of your practice.

If you've got your network to the point where it's routinely delivering interesting and increasingly lucrative projects for you then why would you lock up a bunch of days at a rate lower than you might get elsewhere?

Conversely, isn't there some old cliché about birds and bushes?

My response to this particular procurement team won't by now surprise you, but it did surprise them.

I think I was reasonably gracious (☺) in acknowledging what they, no doubt, considered to be a totally reasonable request in return for guaranteed income but went on to explain that if they wanted to lock me out of the market for that much time then contrary to offering a volume discount, I'd need to charge a premium!

They were a little taken aback to say the least as it wasn't something they'd heard a supplier say before, but in the end they got it.

In the forthcoming year I did more days with them than the procurement team had offered to guarantee and I protected, actually even increased, my relative rate.

PRO TIP

Don't Be Tempted to Drop Your Price

Sticking to your guns on price is critical. If they want you, they want you. That doesn't give you licence to charge anything you like, but defending your premium rate is something you'll never regret. However, when your price has gone down once it's both very difficult to get it back up again and highly likely that they'll ask again.

TOOLKIT

So, let's get into the detail of producing a compelling proposal that will have your potential client swooning, their bosses agreeing and the moolah flowing.

1. Format

I produce proposals in one of five formats:

a.   Simple email

Used in situations where the client wants to move fast, where they've hired me multiple times before and/or where it's just a small initial engagement. Around a third of my engagements are proposed this way.

b.   PowerPoint®

The most common format I use. It forces me to make it easy to read and affords the opportunity to develop an appealing and engaging overall look. Always saved and sent as a PDF to protect the fonts and formatting.

c.   Word®

Used less and less frequently as it feels old fashioned and creates a wall of text that time-poor clients are less likely to read. Trigger for use is where I'm aware that this is the format they prefer. Again, always saved and sent as a PDF.

d. Illustrator®

Very early on I found that producing beautiful documents that go beyond what anyone can do on
standard programmes is a professional skill, and so
I've long worked with a talented freelance graphic designer. He's got to know my preferences and
foibles and is brilliant at translating my scrawls and
scribbles into really impressive visualisations. I use
him for about 1 in 20 of my complete proposals,
though it's rare that he doesn't produce at least one
of the graphics of every proposal I send. Worth his
weight in gold – just don't tell him that...

Please also don't tell him but I did once download various components of Adobe Creative Cloud in the deluded belief I could do it myself. For the same reason
that I don't do my own year-end accounts, I soon de-
leted the trial versions and went back to enjoying the
freedom that hiring a real professional affords you.

e. RFP reply

A couple of times per quarter, we get invited to par-
ticipate in formal procurement processes and these
generally stipulate a pre-defined format. Though we
often no-bid these (where we haven't been involved
in discussions prior to the RFP issuance), when we
do submit a response we grudgingly accept that the
spreadsheet or online service intentionally allows for

little creativity. We understand that some organisations prefer (indeed, some governmental organisations are mandated) to work in this way and so we do our best to comply with the process, hoping we can get past these mass auditions and out to judges' houses as soon as possible.

2. Discussion document

There's a really interesting type of situation where the discussion you're having with the potential client is definitely about a 'real thing' but where money isn't being discussed at all. These are often interactions where 'the potential client want' has developed over a series of conversations but where our contact needs to sell-in the idea of bringing in outside help.

If we fail in our efforts to encourage our contact to let us meet more people (and wow them with our genius) or perhaps where we've met some of the people but the ones with the real authority are just out of reach, then we might suggest a discussion document. In essence, these are the same as a proposal, just without anything on costs and perhaps more optionality than a final proposal.

In the right circumstances these can be a fantastic, high value chess move that once you've got approval the final money stage becomes significantly easier.

I use this kind of device around once per quarter and I can't recall the last time it didn't ultimately turn into an engagement.

3. Executive Summary

Particularly complex, large or very senior stakeholder proposals benefit enormously from an Executive Summary as the first page. Always written last, the Executive Summary takes every element of the proposal and summarises it in four to six paragraphs of no more than 400–500 words.

'Every element' means including the price. I've read hundreds of so-called Executive Summaries that were in fact no more than a vacuous and self-important introduction to the proposal. As French mathematician and philosopher Blaise Pascal wrote in 1657 (not Mark Twain as often misattributed) 'I have made this longer than usual because I have not had time to make it shorter'.

Synthesising large amounts of information into readable prose is a tough but important skill to develop (as you've been reading here, I've still plenty of development needed). Executive Summaries are great practice. I write a proposal that warrants one around twice per year.

Visit the Positive Momentum Network at:

www.positivemomentum.com/network.

There you will find a step-by-step breakdown of the Positive Momentum Proposal Structure to really walk you through everything you need to focus on to ensure that your proposal has the best possible chance of success.

Once we've worked through all of the elements, re-read it three times, had a grammar pedant review it and corrected all the howlers, then we click send and wait...

In fact, you know what we do next, right? That's right, we go work on something else and let this one propagate.

I tend not to chase for a response until at least five working days have passed and, typically, I don't ever directly chase at all. I just can't bear how desperate those *'just wondering if you got my proposal?'* emails sound.

Instead, I send something – typically a printed article that I've read somewhere – that I think the potential client might find interesting and is relevant to the challenge that they might like me to help address for them.

Clients, of course, know why I'm sending something.

They know it's a none too subtle nudge, but you know what? It generally works and gets the dialogue going again, even if it's not what I want to hear.

As I said before, by the time you get to this stage there are a huge number of variables that you just can't control. Once that proposal is gone, you've pretty much done all you can, so don't sit there refreshing your inbox or checking the Wi-Fi connection.

Throw another log on the fire.

SUMMARY

I've wept over too many potential engagements lost at the final stage just because the consultant didn't think strategically enough about how to secure the deal.

They thought they were there before they actually were. They took their eye off the ball and got complacent. Their contact convinced them that all was well and this final stage was just a formality.

The global consulting industry is estimated to be worth around $250 billion per annum. The market is completely established, it's growing and your expertise is in ever-increasing demand.

People who call themselves consultants and who have less experience and competency than you are getting hired for big bucks by organisations every day.

How come? Well, amongst other things, they know how to secure the deal.

They can put together a proposal and investment plan that's beguiling and seductive because it's all about the client. They make themselves incredibly easy to do business with. They play every angle until the purchase order number arrives. And of course they don't cheapen and demean themselves by pushing hard because they're working on lots of other opportunities.

If you're going to go to all the effort outlined in previous chapters (and I really hope you are), please don't blow it by failing to take this stage seriously.

Only go to the effort of a proposal when you are certain the prospective client will really value it.

- ☑ Focus on playing back a beautifully synthesised version of the prospective client's context.

- ☑ Invest effort in the aesthetic – and make that client focused too.

- ☑ Always talk investment, never cost, fee or rates.

- ☑ Keep your propaganda to the minimum.

- ☑ Consider a discussion document as a useful chess move.

Get free resources on sealing the deal

The Positive Momentum Network will give you more tips and advice related to sealing the deal, along with other resources, information and support for independent consultants. Sign up for free at
www.positivemomentum.com/network

CHAPTER 9

Delivering

Quality Counts

One evening, over dinner after a tough workshop with his team, a client said to me, *'You should really meet my wife...'*

Turns out that she had just exited corporate life after a very successful career in the information services industry and had set up her own consulting business. I was happy to meet with her (as I have with hundreds of others) to help a fellow consultant on their way but within half an hour was determined that she come and join Positive Momentum.

Alison was then, and remains today, the most polished and best prepared consultant I've ever had the privilege to work with. Her planning spreadsheets are legendary; she builds contingency buffers into every client deliverable and she even makes audio recordings when people are giving her advice and then transcribes them so as not to miss a thing!

I realise I'm making her sound very geeky and control-freaky here (and if she approves me publishing her story I'll be amazed) but she's also one of the warmest, most engaging, calm and generous people I've the honour to call both a colleague and a friend.

During various major client projects, she and I have travelled all over Europe, often on very early morning and late night flights. As you'll know if you've travelled similarly, these short-haul flights can be unpredictable and delay ridden and on many occasions she and I have been stuck in airport lounges surrounded by lots of grumpy and self-important businesspeople getting agitated with circumstances they are powerless to control. Alison never ever complains and is always great company despite the fact that I'm frequently aware her personal plans are being thrown into disarray by the late incoming flight from wherever.

This demeanor very much extends to her dealings with clients. In more than one joint pitch meeting I've felt her warning glare across the table as a procurement person asks a question designed to provoke me. Well before I 'react' she answers with charm and respect. Throughout engagements, and no matter how obstinate someone in a client team decides to be (adverse reactions to our advice is a constant occupational hazard), she builds positive and enduring relationships at all levels.

She produces client material that always impresses. Whether it's a training deck, a consulting report or simply general client email correspondence, it will be faultless, contemporary and engaging. Aesthetics in materials matter and Alison knows how to work with our designer to really hit that spot with clients.

Not only does she have all of these qualities but she's also a fantastic public servant. The criminal justice system in the UK relies on a lower court called the Magistrates Court. Magistrates are members of the public specially trained to make judgements in an incredibly diverse range of very unfortunate situations; indeed 95% of all UK criminal cases are either heard or at least begin in a Magistrates Court.

Alison's motivation for being a magistrate is pure public service. But this interesting and impressive aspect of her existence is currency in conversations with clients. Having another aspect to your brand, one where you help others in society in some way, for no personal gain, both differentiates and educates you in unimaginable ways.

For all these reasons, Alison is the epitome of delivering distinctively and sets a standard to which we all aspire. In fact, a few years ago she decided to step away from consulting to spend more time with family and friends and to build an amazing new home in the rural East Midlands of the UK. Whilst we miss her professionally, the true measure of how very good she was is that to this day potential clients still contact her about helping them. Longevity of client relationships is the real measure of excellence in the consulting game and Alison was world class.

MYTHBUSTERS

You've only gone and done it!

You've got the gig and the invoice is logged in the client's accounting system ready to be paid. Now the real work starts, but happily from now on you're being rewarded. Better than that, this could be the start of something that extends beyond the current scope and/or opens up a new avenue of your network that could serve you for years to come.

But, dangers abound.

The spotlight is now really on. Expectations are high. The sceptics are preparing hidden traps. The bean-counters want to see an early return on their investment. Your sponsor is praying that they've done the right thing and you're going to make them look good.

This is your moment.

It's first night on Broadway, the critics are on the front row and there's no room for mistakes. But let's not peek nervously around the curtains. Let's stride onto stage with confidence in our experience. Let's grab the audience by the throat from the first bar and work diligently toward a standing ovation at the end of the engagement.

Too many consultants start out engagements on the wrong foot – and never recover. They don't tune into the culture, network and politics of their clients quickly enough. They suck up to the execs and treat others with disdain. They act as if they're somehow the client's saviour. They don't show value quickly enough. Their 'insight' is derivative and obvious. Their output isn't polished, usable and distinct enough. As projects come to a close their scope miraculously starts to creep as they attempt to build co-dependence.

In short, they reinforce every negative stereotype that's alive and well about blood sucking, superior, self-serving consultants.

Being distinctive therefore is much easier than it should be.

Simply, be more Alison...

"

Don't think for a minute that you now have some free licence to say what you like to whoever you like whenever you like.

"

MINDSET

Be careful what you say

Just because the client has now agreed to pay you for your genius, don't think for a minute that you now have some free licence to say what you like to whoever you like whenever you like.

Hiring you will probably have put some noses out of joint. Some of those noses will at this point be unknown to you. Threats to your existence lurk in the organisational undergrowth and believing that your sponsor will protect you is delusional – no matter how bombproof they claim to be.

I know that I've been a jerk with many more than one person inside a client and it's always been to my cost. A certainty on the right solution and a confidence about sponsor air cover have too often led to arrogance, even outright dismissiveness of the opinions and ideas of others inside the client team.

This isn't about whether my ideas were right or wrong. It's all about relationships and you're going to find that these are either the greatest accelerator or the greatest inhibitor to your long-term success.

A maxim I've always tried to remember is that 'you can be right or you can be happy' and whilst matters are rarely this binary, consultants do, by nature, rather have a tendency to want to be right all the time, sometimes to our cost.

Now, I suspect at this point some readers will be getting all up themselves about integrity and authenticity and all that. Please don't muddy this point with polarising high-mindedness. No one is suggesting you shouldn't act with integrity. Just don't be a know-it-all. There's enough of them in the world already, and take it from one who I know has been quite rightly called out for these behaviors, it's not good for your wealth.

TOOLKIT

Every engagement will have its own unique story. How you win it, how you deliver it and how it concludes will never be the same twice.

In our final toolkit, I'm going to lay out in detail the essential steps of the early honeymoon stages of the engagement, the sometimes hard yards of the main work and the moment you'll mostly dread (but occasionally pray for) – the end.

1. Beginning

Really, really do your homework before you start. Clients will choose you once because they feel you've got special expertise. They'll choose you again and again and again because you've worked hard to really, truly understand them.

Invest the time in going back to their website, their investor site if they've got one, tracking their news updates and reviewing as many LinkedIn profiles and documents you can get them to send you as humanly possible. Last time we looked at all this we were focused on the win. This time it's different.

PRO TIP
Get Uncomfortable

Whatever your domain area, go research somewhere else. If sales is your thing, then go spend some time in their operational environment; if IT is your thing, then go and spend some time with their marketeers. Wherever you would be least comfortable, head there.

Never be arrogant and think you are good enough to learn it as you go. It's never a risk worth taking and it means a lot to them if you have taken the time to be involved.

a. **Immerse yourself in their business fast – learn their language**

Open your eyes and ears as wide as possible and ask about everything. Rediscover the curiosity of a child and allow your client to educate you in the past, present and future of their business.

Ask about stuff that might not seem to have anything to do with your brief and always, always understand the commercial performance of the business so that everything you do can be connected to the company's challenges and goals at the highest level. Remember the CFO Test? You passed the first paper but unannounced spot checks from stakeholders are common. Be ready.

By remaining objective and with a wide perspective, you will gather knowledge that will earn you the right to have an opinion.

b. Get 'interviewed' by as many people as you can to gain buy-in and credibility

No doubt you will have one or two brilliant sponsors who are promoting your profile in the organisation. As your gateway and ambassador they are invaluable in establishing your credibility.

Unless they're not.

The reality is that your presence will very likely be threatening to some people, and unless your initial interaction with them is as positive as possible, they could easily turn into enemies later down the track, ready to ambush you when the slightest hiccup occurs.

A great technique is to ask your sponsors to ask others involved to meet and 'interview' you and give their opinion as to the best approach for the project. Your sponsors may be reticent at first and will probably explain that they don't care whether certain parties want you there or not. This is high risk and the people who you most want to be interviewed by are the ones that your sponsor is least inclined to listen to! Coach your sponsor on the psychology behind this and get them to see the value in this long-game approach. Most importantly, quickly build a relationship with as many people as you can and get them to feel comfortable with you.

c. Build brilliant relationships – buy lunches, connect on LinkedIn, help for nothing

Whether it's the receptionist in their head office, the 'at-risk' project leader that you are there to 'help', or the VP of Sales, everyone needs your best side and a sense that you are there to help them personally.

Despite the pressure, make time for the chat over coffee, the quiet sandwich together (that you pay for), the support for something they are struggling with, or just the simple exchange of business cards and connection on LinkedIn.

Everything you do establishes their perception of your personality in their mind. As brilliant as you are at fixing stuff, never underestimate the deadly power of someone junior, who is better connected than you know, not liking you.

d. Be on-site and highly visible as much as possible

Client's priorities have a nasty habit of changing – a lot – and if you are not frequently visible it's extremely easy to lose track of what is going on.

Whilst you don't want to be just hanging around with no particular purpose, asking big clients if they mind if you use their premises sometimes for catching up with other work often goes a very long way. It makes them feel important and that they somehow are top of your list. Find somewhere to base yourself where you know there will be a lot of footfall and where the chance of innocently running into people is maximised.

For those dangerous stakeholders who believe that consultants are expensive and add little value, it's vital to be visible, which will help remind them that you are connected and adding value. Being remote quickly diminishes your credibility.

e. Keep your counsel early on – ask great questions but don't show off

You're called in as the saviour of a big project that's going badly wrong. It's bang in your sweet spot and you know exactly what to do. At the first meeting they share the full horror of the current situation and then all (or at least most) eyes turn to you and await your words of wisdom that will surely dig them all out of the pit they have got themselves into.

Feeling confident and self-assured, you prepare in your mind a dazzling few sentences that will have them all swooning, perhaps even considering a few flamboyant sweeps of the pen on the whiteboard...

and then you remember. This is just a first meeting. You don't really know what's going on yet or who is really who. You keep your ego in check and instead engage the meeting in a great discussion based on some really good, neutral questions.

You have averted the disaster that often befalls the cocky consultant. Bravo! Give them what they want and earn the right to give them what they need.

f. Find trusted allies with whom to test your early views and ideas

Most organisations are a complicated but largely hidden tangle of politics, opinions and egos. In the early stages you need to take very great care not to become ensnared by these hidden traps.

Despite your experience and the inevitable feeling that you've seen this all before, treading carefully with your early ideas will pay massive dividends when you actually need to get stuff done later on. Build a diverse network of influential individuals at all levels and with whom you can discreetly bounce ideas around. Far better to sense resistance one-to-one when you are simply floating a draft idea off the back of a napkin in a coffee shop, than to experience the tumbleweed moment of an ill-thought-through presentation in front of a group of hassled execs, many of whom arrive ready to disagree with anything you say simply because you are a consultant.

g. Beware 'false protection' – stakeholders always protect themselves first

One of the biggest dangers you'll face is the stakeholder(s) who tells you to be provocative and shake things up and who promises you protection from any consequences.

Don't believe a word of it!

This kind of talk plays brilliantly to our egos and our inherent desire to go and make a big difference really quickly. No matter what level someone is, their ability to protect a mere consultant from hostility created early on is virtually zero, not least because they will need to protect their own reputation first.

Many a consultant has been shot down before they even started as a result of protection that mysteriously disappeared on the field of battle. Instead, take early engagements very carefully, and with all your might resist the urge to blurt out pronouncements until you really know what is what and who is who.

h. Gently remind people that you're NOT an employee – talk about other clients

Paradoxically, one of the most positive compliments you can get is when a client treats you like a part of the core team. It's a paradox because it really shows that you have done a great job in establishing yourself within the client, but once people think you are full-time they will treat you as such and flood you with boring meeting requests and massive distribution list emails about trivia.

Part of you – that old corporate part – might even like the feeling of being back as part of a team and the delusion of security you get lulled into believing it offers. Fight it! Remind people that you shouldn't be sitting in routine meetings. Casually name drop the other clients and projects you are working on – even if these are only at the vague discussion stage.

Really do anything to stop you, and them, slipping into the comfortable slipper of routine employment – unless of course that's what you want, in which case you never know, the project might turn into a job.

i. Resist 'employee assets' – email addresses, laptops etc.

Assuming that you don't actually want a job, then it makes sense to resist items that are normally the preserve of full-time employees. Once you have a door pass, an email address and even a laptop you really have become part of the furniture.

Apart from the logistical challenge of having to keep all of these items safe and remembering to bring them with you each time you are with this client, you've really got to evaluate whether having them is a nice or a need to have. You might occasionally find yourself engaged in a project where security is a major issue and where holding some of these items is unavoidable. However, the minute you've got them permanently, that's when they will start to think and treat you like you're permanent – except without any of the benefits!

Treat each situation on its merits, but if you want to be an independent consultant, then emphasise your independence. The key point here is time efficiency, and not killing yourself with multiple emails, diaries and mobile phones. The best way to keep your sanity is to avoid their systems and platforms.

2. Middle

a. Organisation charts are your friend – gather and constantly monitor

Everyone loves a good org-chart, right? People love seeing where they are in the pecking order and how big their empire is versus one of their peers. Most of our clients are littered with these posters to vanity, and they can be incredibly helpful to us.

Many of the issues that occur in corporate life are as a result of the interactions, shared accountabilities, hand-offs, chasms, silos and politics between people and functions. Make it your mission to master the matrix of your client and understand how all these pieces fit (or perhaps don't) together. Org-charts are the fastest and easiest way to get a grip of this, and so, every time you meet someone new, ask them for a copy of their team's org-chart, and to talk you through who is who. Remember also, that everyone loves a good re-org, and so the org-chart you have today won't necessarily still be true tomorrow.

This is very much a constant task, even if you work with the same client for years. All of your clients are fundamentally people businesses and knowing your way around will mean you can keep one step ahead, all of the time.

b.   Be aware but detached from the politics – stay outside looking in by being inside looking out

You probably left corporate life to get away from all of the politics, and so the idea of having to lower yourself back into that murky pool is possibly quite distasteful. The challenge is that the very reason we are often brought in is because the politics has created a situation where outsiders are considered the only way forward. Many consultants claim to be above the politics and feel that because they are independent, then all the political stuff does not matter to them.

Well, if you like short engagements and a bad reputation, then of course you can continue to labour under this misapprehension. If, instead, you do this to eat and pay the mortgage, then knowing what's going on behind closed doors really matters, for your survival, as much as the chances of delivering what you have been hired to do. Keep your ears and eyes open. Look out for the cliques and cabals. Make friends with all of them and build a reputation for being incredibly discreet.

TRAP TO AVOID
Don't Get Drawn into Gossip

The minute you run back to your key sponsor with the latest gossip is the minute that your reputation is blown – not just with the person who gossiped with you, but possibly with your sponsor too. Avoid the temptation to take sides and as a result risk biting the hand that feeds you. Be discreet, tactful and impartial always.

c. Build a following and fan base, especially among the junior staff

Since you're not trying to build a career in your client – you're not are you? – you can afford to be nice to everyone. You might not think much of what the people in the business have achieved, but showing that in any way, shape or form means that you haven't understood that your key sponsor will offer you far less protection than they are promising if they had to make a choice between themselves and you.

There will be plenty of people who will want to goad you into joining their little campaign against another division or person. Be wise and rise above it. Listen empathetically to what they have to say, but never, ever take sides – unless of course you are independently wealthy and only doing this for fun. The most important people to build a following with are perhaps counter-intuitively the most junior.

You have no idea how much influence the grumpy receptionist has, and so treating them poorly is a gamble that's just not worth taking. Instead, take an interest in what everyone has to say, and remember simple things about them to deepen that relationship every day. Today's junior salesperson is tomorrow's CEO, and you'll likely still want work in 10 years' time. They won't forget your kindness when they have budget to spend. Make sure everyone thinks you are a good person.

d. Choose your moments and people to challenge incredibly carefully

As we've said repeatedly, you need to take your time before shooting your mouth off, but you can only keep your powder dry for so long. Sooner or later someone is going to expect you to say something provocative and, whilst few of us need any encouragement, you might need a reminder to be careful with your timing and method from time-to-time.

The best way to start the more challenging dialogues is one-to-one and in a tentative manner that gives you the possibility to hit reverse should the response be in any way hostile. The reality is that we are often lifting the carpet tiles to some rather unpleasant discoveries, and it's all too easy to shoot the messenger, i.e. you.

So be a smart messenger and consider carefully how, when and with whom you will raise things. Ideally, call another consultant that you know and trust who isn't involved, tell them about it and ask them how they might address it. Members of the Positive Momentum community often tell me that this is one of the biggest value adds they get: the chance to rehearse and road test the most challenging moments in our client relationships.

We go in to fix things. We owe the client a candid view. However, we also don't need to be a bull in a china shop and an extra few hours of contemplation rarely makes any difference to anything. Act in haste, repent at leisure.

e. Take care to stay focused on their delivery agenda and not build your own

This is your biggest moment. Your main job is to deliver something and not doing this well is the biggest reason consultants get a bad name. As you really start to get under the bonnet, you will inevitably start to form your own opinion of what should be done, when and by whom. Very likely your client will ask for your view on this, possibly even asking you to come up with a timeline and series of deliverables.

This is yet another danger zone where care and consideration are critical. Perhaps you and your sponsor feel this project can be delivered in six weeks, whereas everyone else thinks it's twelve. Sticking with your sponsor won't help you much when they get fired after eight weeks; however, siding with everyone else against your sponsor won't do you any good either. Instead, be seen as the peacemaker who works with all parties to develop a workable delivery agenda that everyone can live with, and then drive that agenda as much as you possibly can.

Two of the biggest criticisms of consultants are scope creep and timeline slide. Many clients feel (often quite rightly) that consultants do this to maximise their billing. Be different. Remember that reputation is all, and always, always do what you say you will do.

f. Make sure all of your work reflects their language and tone

Having done these kinds of projects a time or two before, you'll have developed your own shorthand way of describing what you do. You might even have inherited some methodologies that you believe are important disciplines to follow when engaging in a project. And you might be right. Trouble is if that language or approach is alien to how the client thinks, you've an uphill battle from the start.

TRAP TO AVOID
Don't Be a Show Off

Don't show off your black belt, five–star project management approach too early. It's intimidating, irritating and might not work in this context. It's said that if you want to start a revolution it's best to start small, and that's always the best way with what we do. Start by learning their language and jargon and reflect what you do in this style. Certainly, gently nudge them toward better practices, but don't be the smart-alec outsider banging on, as you might just find yourself further outside than is good for your bank balance. Learn to be a chameleon and adapt your approach to theirs – using their language.

g. Show how your work is progressing with impressive visuals

One of our Positive Momentum hallmarks is our ability to be able to synthesise and bring to life our work in impressive visual formats. Whether it's a timeline or a project overview, making just a little extra effort with the polish and production of these can really set you apart. Better still, they are an awesome way of getting further work, as these get shown around inside your client.

It's unlikely, however, that you consider yourself much of a Picasso, and so will likely need some help in getting these just how you want them. That's where help from a professional graphic designer, as we've suggested before, comes in to play. All you need to do is scribble something on a piece of paper, take a picture and email it to them and they will work their magic. They might not get it right first time, but by the second or third attempt you'll be amazed at what they can produce.

Make sure to deliver something quickly with high impact. Clients rarely expect much early on, which only serves to reinforce their sometimes dim view of consultants. Do the opposite and give them the wow factor early.

This is one of those areas that isn't at all a 'need to do', but in terms of future business it's a whole lot more valuable than a 'nice to do' as well.

h. Communicate brilliantly with clarity, context and character – plan and rehearse

Depending on the nature of the engagement, you might need to justify your existence with written updates, one-to-one reviews and perhaps even the odd group presentation.

This is one place where just being as good as you were in corporate life won't be enough.

The big global consultancies take this part of 'the dance' super seriously and rehearse the hell out of any set piece presentation. Whilst you don't want to produce the 150-page slide decks of our massive counterparts, you do need to deliver your message brilliantly, memorably and with conviction.

It all starts with being able to synthesise the complex simply. One page is better than ten. A poster is better than a slide. A cleverly produced visual is better than a bit of low-rent PowerPoint SmartArt.

Next up comes the client's context. The more your update relates what you are doing to their overall business objectives – client, revenue etc. – the better, even if your stakeholder isn't that well informed on these matters. Give them something to make themselves look brilliant in front of their boss.

Remember that the messenger matters as much as the message. Let your personality show. Learn a little showmanship, if you don't feel you have enough, and make sure there is just the right amount of theatre in what you reveal.

One last thing. You might have been a last-minute-Charlie in corporate life, but if you think you can wing it with this stuff as an independent consultant you will find yourself sorely (and expensively) mistaken.

i.   Frequently do stuff that they would not expect, but really value

Sadly, just delivering on the original project objectives won't be enough to secure future work for you. That's the minimum expectation, and though no doubt it will be hard fought, it will equally be easily forgotten.

What clients really remember are the things you did for them that they never even asked for. That brilliant candidate for a role they were struggling to fill; that fascinating article buried deep within a magazine they subscribe to, but never have time to read; that introduction to a potential new client; that work experience placement for their son or daughter that you arranged; or that presentation for their boss that no one but you and they knows you actually wrote.

Whatever it might be, going the extra mile by thinking about the needs of the people you are working with – even the ones you don't like much – will go an incredibly long way and will pay you back for many, many years to come.

j. Use technology consciously to stay visible when you are not there

As we've said throughout this book, visibility is key and that's especially true as the client starts signing off your invoices.

A quick email or text when you know a key event is occurring for your client or stakeholder can work wonders in keeping you front of mind and reinforcing the value you are adding. Equally, jumping on a video call can really help to keep your presence felt in a much more tangible way. Using LinkedIn daily also helps to make sure that your name and face keeps popping up and reminding everyone at the client of your existence. It's amazing how little effort maintaining visibility takes when you master the technology that works for each client.

k. Be different to normal blood-sucking consultants – talk about when it's over

You don't want a job with them, do you? But you do like the monthly retainer that you've managed to negotiate and life without it would look just a little bleaker... Hmm, tricky, huh? It's lovely having a client that keeps on giving, but as we all know, consultants can be easily stereotyped into ambulance-chasing takers who will do anything just to cut another invoice.

The real danger is that you cut back on the C2C meetings elsewhere and get slowly lulled into a horrible false sense of security only to find that your project gets cut just when you least expected it.

Whilst we all think it will never happen to us, most independent consultants have been through this – the really successful ones several times!

The only way to avoid this is to take control of the situation and actively engage in discussions about when the arrangement will be over.

It takes bravery, but client respect is guaranteed even if it can feel a little bit like splitting up with a partner. Call it reverse psychology if you like, but the weird thing is that with many clients the more you push away, the more they will draw you to them. Or they won't, and you get to go find a newer, more lucrative, possibly even more grateful, client.

3. End

a. Keep yourself focused on task completion – don't be a magpie

With our favoured style of getting in under the radar on smaller projects that others might pass over, we are naturally interested, sometimes even anxious, to discover the next opportunity inside the client.

Of course with larger clients the opportunities are often numerous. It can feel like walking into an Aladdin's cave of consulting treasure and our avarice for more can quickly get out of control.

Beware!

Everything relies on that first (or indeed current) gig, no matter how small and insignificant it might seem to you. Drive it through to completion brilliantly and keep yourself focused on project completion, even if the last bits are quite boring. Be crystal clear about what needs to be delivered, set and manage expectations and stay focused, deliver it and do it well. Nothing else matters until it's done and try to avoid tinkering with it to ensure you do it in time and without it taking over your life.

Clients of course will often be the biggest magpie behaviour sinners, so be very aware of them seducing you with the bright lights of the next possible project and instead assure them of your interest, but help them to stay disciplined on completion. Employees can often get away with starting something and then not finishing it – we most definitely cannot and will pay a heavy price if we try to do so.

b. **In every way imaginable, demonstrate the value delivered**

Clients easily lose track of the value a project was intended to deliver. One project gets superseded by another and more often than not clients fail to recognise either the failings or successes of the effort undertaken by their teams.

Since we are not encumbered with many of the issues that cause such inertia for them – quarterly reporting, career to worry about, next year's budget, idiot in the team etc. – we are free to focus on how what we are doing delivers business results.

Be the person who stays resolutely focused on the expected outcomes of the work and find any and every way to highlight how well it's delivering commercially. Take the initiative and reach out into other functions who are seeing the fruits of your labour and report back (or even better get *them* to report back) on the progress that's being experienced. You know this organisation's key KPIs, right? So track them diligently and compare the historical picture with where you are today and make sure that everyone involved gets the right amount of recognition

– yourself included! As you have expertly built a virtual team to deliver (you have, right?) make sure you shout from the hills about what the team has done, as often as possible.

c. Work out how to finish on a spectacular high

You might not exactly arrange a fourth of July firework spectacular to conclude your efforts, but thinking about the finale of your show will go a very, very long way to cementing your reputation with all the stakeholders and spectators, with obvious long-term benefits for you.

Of course it depends very much on the nature of your assignment as to what is appropriate, but having a plan is key. Whether it's a grand unveiling of a new system or approach, the conclusion of a programme or the completion of a build to hand over to a business-as-usual team, the theatre of the finish is something really worth thinking about. Arranging a gathering of key players in a particular environment could be right, designing a really special handover binder might be just what they need, or maybe even thinking about how you launch something new to the rest of the business with just a little extra pizzazz could be enough. Whatever happens, just make sure that your ending doesn't fizzle like a damp rocket on a wet evening and instead sparkles like a star in the sky that everyone remembers.

d. Build an inner circle to hand the keys over to

You just can't start thinking about this soon enough. As we've said repeatedly, fighting the desire to make your client dependent on you is the major inner battle we all face.

One of the easiest ways to overcome this and keep ourselves honest is to build an inner circle of full-timers who can pick up and run with our work. Don't be over choosy and instead remember they have a career to pursue and bosses to please and so it's our place to equip them with the processes and skills to be able to outshine us – whether you would have recruited them or not.

Build this coalition quickly and tell them explicitly that you want to enable them to get the spotlight and to run with things successfully long after you've gone. Then tell others that that is what you are doing and get their counsel and help in doing so.

As with all leadership, empowerment creates followership and whether this is following you in taking over your masterpiece or following you to the next project really does not matter.

e. Build an exit plan and share it widely

With an inner circle in place, ready and willing to take the keys, you can now start openly discussing your exit. Privately at first with your key sponsor, but rapidly thereafter with a much wider community.

The sooner it's recognised that you don't see yourself as a permanent feature, the sooner barriers can be eliminated in those who are threatened by you – and if you are any good, there will likely be many who are.

The timing of this conversation will vary from project to project. Some clients want you to be explicit and public on this from day minus one, others act like jilted lovers at the very suggestion. Whatever the circumstance, keep your radar highly attuned to any even slight indications that others think you're getting a bit too comfy and respond rapidly with exit proposals.

Exit plans vary in shape and form but they all have one thing in common: a date! You and the client need something to work toward so that all of the consequences of your departure can be planned for – both the consequences for the client and for you. Whether you need to hire someone to do your role full-time or simply document everything you've done so that others can pick it up easily in the future, it all serves to cement both in your mind and the clients that all good things must come to an end.

f. Look out for phony projects cooked up just 'cos they like having you around

Just like the athlete that wants to end their career on a gold medal win, so you too should want to end your time with a client on a genuinely transformational piece of work.

The consequence of developing fantastic interpersonal skills is that clients really like us. Remember Jamie from Chapter 6? This is an overwhelmingly good thing, unless it results in them giving us soft, meaningless projects just to keep us around. Whilst tempting for your bank balance, the damage to your reputation can be considerable. In a heartbeat you can go from being seen as a guru to only being viewed as a rented drinking buddy for your sponsor. Don't ever let your sponsor feel they need to find you something else. Keep them appraised of all the other potential clients you are talking to – you are, aren't you? – and tell them that they really don't need to find you other things as you are much in demand elsewhere, even if you aren't just yet.

Of course the real danger here is that you end up diluting all the good you have done by taking something vague on as a favour in your spare time. Simply don't do it.

g. Keep your ego in control – of course they love you, but you don't want a job, do you?

'You're the best consultant we've ever had', 'Your ideas are pure genius', 'We just could not have done any of this without you'. These are all statements we (hope to) hear from clients in the moments after the successful completion of a project. They are in that heady moment of euphoria where briefly all their problems seem to have been blown away and it's all because of their shining star that is the very brilliant you!

This is the moment where the gravity of a full-time role with all the so-called benefits will be at its greatest. This is the moment where you are most vulnerable to the ultimate step in their courting of you. And perhaps you will yield to their offer. Perhaps you will go back to corporate life, love it, do brilliantly, and never look back. Many have, and if you do, then good for you. However, many have also regretted it six months later and realised they were duped by their own ego, seduced by their own self-importance and persuaded by the deluded promise to themselves that it will all be so different this time.

Our advice will always be to step away and take some time to think. Let that euphoric moment pass and see if it still looks so good in the cold light of day. If it does, then good luck to you and may I buy you a coffee sometime soon?

h. Let others take full credit – they have a career to consider, you don't

As projects come to a conclusion it's human nature to seek recognition for the effort you have put in. All those tough deadlines, harsh budgets and political dancing you had to do surely now deserves some public appreciation. Isn't it now time that those inept people on or around the programme finally got their comeuppance? Those so-called project colleagues who you suspect were silently stabbing you in the back and protecting their own backsides while you worked all hours... revenge would be so sweet, wouldn't it? Well, it might be sweet initially, but as the ripples of your pride reach out and damage your reputation, the taste will very soon turn sour, and in ways you will never know, but that will reduce the frequency that the phone rings. Just a little doubt is enough to strangle new opportunities long before they reach your radar.

But you're not that dumb.

You will be quietly making sure that everyone involved gets all the credit – maybe even more than they deserve – while you quietly and humbly play down your part. At least you will if you like money...

i. Keep networking – it never mattered more than now

Often the final stages of a project offer an opportunity for some accelerated networking as a wider community becomes involved in the work you have been doing in darkened rooms for many months.

Refocus your networking spirit, make sure you are loaded up with business cards every day and get the credit card whirring with some lunches and dinners. It's critical that you don't become totally defined by the project you have just delivered. Clients love to put us in a box and, whilst it can help, it's far more likely to be limiting in terms of future opportunities. Just as you would with any brand new contact, get the conversation off what you have done and on to their business challenges as soon as you can. Expand and redirect the dialogue, be more interested than interesting, ask a few well-informed BGQs and notice how quickly they see that you are so much more than the brilliant project you have just delivered.

j. Make yourself redundant – and get out

So you've told them you're leaving them. You've packed your things and given back your pass – what were you doing with that by the way?! You've made sure that the handover was neat and that the key people know how to contact you.

Now, get the hell out of there and for a while at least don't look back. The reality is that nothing is ever fully completed. There will always be a few extra items that need attention, but it's critical that you draw a line and make good on your promise to hand over to the team you have prepared so well. After very intensive or lengthy projects a period of downtime might even be advisable, but you will certainly need to detach as much for your sanity as for the good governance of the project.

k. Do something special/expensive with your key stakeholders

You've obviously worked hard and you might even feel that they got the deal of the century given how much they paid versus the value you delivered. No doubt these feelings are valid, but you have also invoiced a lot of money and your sponsor and other stakeholders probably had to repeatedly justify your fees to their bosses.

PRO TIP
Be Generous

Spending some decent money now on a generous and creative gift and/or an expensive dinner will really help to solidify your reputation as a classy operator. Think about what you have learnt about people as the project has gone on and do something you know they would really appreciate and enjoy. Remember also to include people at all levels as well as some of your adversaries – keep your friends close but your enemies closer, right? Now is not the moment to be tight-fisted. Open up the company wallet and give generously. It will come back to you manyfold.

I. **Stay connected, visible, interested and open to the next brief**

    Put clear blue water between you and the project for sure, but don't disappear entirely. It's one thing to give the impression of being in demand by other clients but taken to extremes you can look like you're not interested.

    Keep your radar firmly on news about the client, use LinkedIn and Google News Alerts to monitor (and react to) key developments. I've gone back to previous clients months and even years later just because of a well-remembered event that I casually contacted an old stakeholder about. We all seek practices that have the protection of multiple clients and the stimulation of new clients, but there is nothing quite like the ease with which you can slip back into the context of a previous client – though of course if you are smart, even with a previous client you will hit the reset button and go straight back to the formula that starts at the beginning of this chapter.

SUMMARY

A great deal of this book intentionally focuses on helping you to attract and win work so that you have a diverse and secure practice that will serve you for the long term.

But the reality is that if you cut corners in your delivery, if your work is unpolished and indistinct, if you're greedy and ungenerous, if you fail to build good relationships even with those who see you as a threat, and if you care more about being right than making things better for the client, then you're making the wrong career choice.

There's a reason that consultants are often not regarded particularly positively. Every organisation has a story of a consulting engagement that didn't deliver for them. Privately, consultants often blame clients for projects that don't work out. Egos abound on both sides of the table – but that creates an opportunity for the likes of you and me.

Being better than average in the consulting industry isn't as hard as it should be, but if you deliver brilliantly in the way I'm advocating here you'll be rewarded with the kind of long-term relationships that will deliver you fascinating, fulfilling and financially rewarding work for as long as you want it – and in Alison's case, for quite a while after too!

☑ Distinctive delivery is the foundation of a sustainable consulting practice.

☑ Keep building the network throughout any engagement.

☑ Keep your friends close and your enemies even closer.

☑ Listen carefully and use extreme tact and careful timing when it's time to give your view.

☑ Never believe that your sponsor(s) will protect you from full-time employees.

☑ Make it clear that this isn't a monogamous relationship.

☑ Start planning your exit early.

Get free resources on delivering effectively

The Positive Momentum Network will give you more tips and advice related to delivering effectively, along with other resources, information and support for independent consultants. Sign up for free at **www.positivemomentum.com/network**

Conclusion

I n case it's not completely obvious by now, I love everything about being an Independent Consultant.

It's the second best decision I've ever made in my life (you know by now that the first was marrying Mrs C) and it has given me the opportunity to work in more places, with more industries and to meet and learn from more amazing people than a life-long conventional career would ever have delivered.

But, for me, that early corporate career was the foundation of the success I've been fortunate to enjoy as a consultant. I believe passionately in the particular value that 'second chapter' consultants deliver for clients and it's why I've written this book. I'm living proof that there is a huge market for former leaders with real-world experience who are willing to be borrowed rather than bought.

The biggest consulting firms in the world lure the best and brightest minds from the world's leading higher education establishments and, you know what, they're amazing. Back when I was an exec, I even hired some of these firms and I rarely regretted it.

But I'm not trying to compete with them, and neither should you.

Where they know the theory, we know the practice and the market is plenty big enough for us all to peacefully coexist.

Where they want the seven-figure engagements with big teams, we're totally happy, even prefer, to engage in a more compact manner.

Where their value is the assurance of their brand, our value is in the triumph and disaster of our experience in the real world.

What we all have in common, though, is the critical importance of building enduring, trusted advisor relationships.

It's people not propositions that fuel sustained success in consulting and I hope I've been able to convince you that the people you already know – and the people who know them – will provide you with more business than you'll ever have enough inventory for.

More than convincing you that you know the people already, I hope I've given you the credible means of reminding them of your genius in ways that won't make you feel like a greasy salesperson. And I hope that I've been able to convince you that no matter what area you specialise in, you can make this work for you.

Clients need you.

Running an organisation in the 21st century is hard and it seems only to be getting harder. The forces of commerce, technology, demographics, geopolitics, climate change, hell even viruses rage in ways we could never have imagined and organisations are increasingly depending on external parties to help them through the constant storm.

Former leaders turned Independent Consultants, with experience just like yours, are being hired right now for thousands a day.

They're doing inspiring work that is changing outcomes for organisations and the people in them.

They're doing all the things they loved about their former full-time roles with much less of the stuff they didn't like/weren't very good at.

The smart ones are working with several clients at the same time, charging premium rates, and so they are enjoying a level of security that no one in a full-time job will ever get anywhere near. And they're spending more time with their family and friends, enjoying their hobbies, giving back to society and living healthier lives than they were before they took this step.

I've lost deals I really wanted, I've had engagements where I didn't achieve what I set out to, I've stayed in some truly terrible hotels, been stuck in airports for much longer than I'd have liked and I've even watched former colleagues become multi-millionaires from their share options, but I've never once regretted the decision to become an Independent Consultant when I did.

I've been at home for every single one of my kids' birthdays, sports days, school productions and every other little never-to-be-repeated event in their lives. I've taken 10+

weeks of holiday every year to coincide with school holidays. I've served my local community and taken much better care of myself than I did in corporate life. I was around in the final years of my parents' lives in a way that I'm certain would have been impossible if I'd had a normal job.

There isn't a single promotion, bonus, equity share, pension plan or fancy office that could ever have got anywhere near making up for the loss of these invaluable things.

I'm not saying it's easy to build a thriving independent consulting practice. I hope that I've made the challenges of choosing this path abundantly clear throughout this book. But I hope that I've also made the recipe for success not just clear and easy to follow but also enticing enough for you to want to try a spoonful too. Now that you have learned my recipe, you should:

▶   Be certain that the time and reasons are right for you to do this

▶   Make sure that those you love are in support

▶   Be open to what others see you as being really good at rather than what you want to be seen as being good at

▶   Learn how to use platforms like LinkedIn to engage intelligently with others and subtly remind them of your genius

- Become well read and always do your research so that you're equipped to have meaningful conversations

- Get out there and ask as many people as you can as often as you can what's going on for them

- Be generous and help people, not because you want something in return but because it's the right thing to do

- C2C your socks off and become an expert in the art of the BGQ

- Take a considered and patient approach – don't push too hard on every door that opens just a crack

- Open many lines of enquiry so you're never depending on too few opportunities

- Use the language of your potential clients and playback their context.

- Be easy to do business with, work pay-as-you-go with the minimum bureaucracy between you and the client

- Develop phenomenal relationships with everyone on the client side – even those who for some inexplicable reason don't seem to love you

- ▶ Deliver with style, distinction and an obsessive focus on making things better (not perfect) for the client.

- ▶ Get better and better, as you become more and more successful, at taking time for rest, relaxation and recharging your mind, body and soul.

Simply stay visible, play chess and deliver distinctively.

Thank you so much for reading and whatever path you choose, I wish for you the freedom, fulfillment and security I've been privileged to enjoy – with of course somewhat fewer unused box files!

If you want more... connect with me.

I'd love to hear from you with comments, questions, ideas and even criticisms of what I've had to say.

I'm as keen to help you succeed as I am to hear your opinion on any of what you've read.

You can email me at **matt.crabtree@positivemomentum.com**, you can follow me on LinkedIn and if you're interested in exploring becoming a Positive Momentum partner you can go to **www.positivemomentum.com/join** and find out more.

Even if that's not for you, we'd love for you to join our Positive Momentum Network at **www.positivemomentum.com/network** where you'll find free material, events and support resources especially curated for anyone wanting to thrive in the wonderful world of independent consulting.

Further Reading

Dare to Lead by Brené Brown

How to Win Friends & Influence People by Dale Carnegie

Good to Great by Jim Collins

The 7 Habits of Highly Effective People by Stephen Covey

The Art of Happiness by His Holiness The Dalai Lama

Slide:ology by Nancy Duarte

Rework by Jason Fried

Outliers by Malcolm Gladwell (plus really anything else he's written)

No Rules Rules by Reed Hastings

The Ride of a Lifetime by Robert Iger

Shoe Dog by Phil Knight

The Five Dysfunctions of a Team by Patrick Lencioni

Turn the Ship Around! by L. David Marquet

What They Don't Teach You at Harvard Business School by Mark McCormack

Lean In by Sheryl Sandberg

Maverick! by Ricardo Semler

Transforming Nokia by Risto Siilasmaa

The Coaching Habit by Michael Bungay Stanier

Thanks for the Feedback by Douglas Stone & Sheila Heen

Black Box Thinking by Matthew Syed

Nudge by Richard H. Thaler & Cass R. Sunstein

Made in America by Sam Walton

Acknowledgements

So many people helped to make this story happen. Growing up on a country estate owned by a Marquess was anything but normal, but my parents, Peter and Marian, and my brothers, Andrew and Ian, were what really made for an amazing childhood, and though I will always be the annoying little brother, their support, counsel and confidence meant and means the world.

The three self-made entrepreneur Tonys that my father befriended helped me see what hard work, determination and optimism could result in. I owe Messrs Turner, Brooker and Ray a lot. As well as Steven and Sagar Woods who gave me my first job on a livestock trading farm – and taught me what real hard work was.

Vince Cugnet gave me that first business book about Lee Iaccoca and then hosted me on his family farm in Zimbabwe in the late 80s. For a lad from the rural midlands, visiting Africa really blew my mind and seeing the sun come up for the first time in 1990 on the South African border is a memory I'll never forget.

My first manager, Andy Beer, took the chance on me that set everything in motion professionally and I'll never be able to thank him enough. He was followed by Eddie Chapman who saved my bacon the first time we met and went on to give me my first shot at management. Cedric

Smith was only briefly my manager but his confidence in me meant a great deal – despite my desertion of him to pastures new. After a difficult first meeting (entirely my fault), Barry Mowbray was the man who more than anyone else taught me what it is to be an outstanding executive leader. He saw something in me that I hadn't seen in myself, he patiently mentored me and together with a group of others we experienced more professionally in four years than most people experience in an entire career. Thank you, Barry.

At Barclays, Chris Lendrum, Alison Hutchinson, Peter Harvey, David Rundle, Roger Davies, Ian Roundell and Jeremy Wilson all helped me much more than my short 18-month sojourn there ever deserved.

Thanks to all those who endured my attempts at leadership in corporate life. To the teams at Pitney Bowes, AT&T, RSL COM and BarclaysB2B and especially to Mike Potter who came to a few of them and even PM for a while, I salute and thank you.

That picture of those seven founding clients, Jeannie Brice, Ashley Blackmore, Andy Oliver, Gary Jennison, Keith Sangwin, Tom Welsh and Will Knights has pride of place on my study wall and always will.

They led to SO many subsequent clients I want to thank and it would take a whole book to credit them all but special mention has to go to Melissa Adams, Steve Allen, Martin Arnold, Birgit Beck, Lara Boro, Diana Breeze,

Nigel Bretton, Alison Brittain, Franz Bruckner, Richard Chapman, Grace Christie, Natasha Christie-Miller, Helen Cockerham, Steve Cooper, Ian Cowie, Richard Dillon, George Eleftheriou, Nick Fahy, John Fawcett, Steve Gee, Camilla Giske, Rukmini Glanard, Tracey Gray, Debbie Griffin, Vinzenz Gruber, Julie Harris, Roy Harris, Andy Hart, Steve Hicks, Michael Howard, Jon Howe, Lucy Johnson, Bernard Johnson, Will Johnston, Evan Jones, Nayan Kisnadwala, Hilmar Kroat-Reder, Francoise Laska, Morten Linnet, Liz Lux, John Lynch, Clare Marchant, Joe Marion, Aileen Markey, Viki Matthews, Brian May, Sarah McCann, Denis McGowan, Penny Mitchell, Joby Mussel, Will Nicol, Jarl Overby, Duncan Painter, Jane Parry, Tiku Patel, Steve Pateman, Tom Pfaff, Mike Randall, Charles Reed, Matteo de Renzi, Lindsey Rix, Richard Rowney, Ana Sanches, Sue Saville, Mark Shashoua, Mairead Sheahan, Claire Silver, Lars Soerbo, Scott Spanton, Suzanne Steele, Keith Stentiford, Georg Storandt, Sepehr Tarverdian, Jill Tennant, Roger Thompson, Andy Vaughan, Kobe Verdonck, Bas Verkooijen, Filip Verstockt, Katy Vu, Tim Waite, Damon Walford, Nick Walker, Nicolas Warchalowski, Amanda Ward, Simon Welling, Penny Williams, Frank van Zanten and Alyona Zhupikova. I know that I've missed so many names. Please forgive me and all know that I'm endlessly grateful.

Without pioneer Positive Momentum partners and support team members this book would never have been written. From the bottom of my heart, thank you to Gary Gamp, Joanna Keeling, Alison Savage, Niall Anderson, Mark Evans, Jamie Malcolm, Linda Armstrong, Rajnish Virmani and Karen Taplin. Your confidence in me so early in our history is humbling. A special mention to former client Chris Savage, first for introducing me to Alison who became a fantastic PM partner and then to them both for helping us to franchise Positive Momentum. True lifelong friends and mentors. To every partner and support team member both past and present, especially our ever-vigilant Finance Manager Estelle, thank you. You've all made Positive Momentum so much more than I could ever have imagined.

Nearly done!

Thank you to my unbelievably brilliant EA, Angela. Your diligence, forethought, attention to detail, client focus and ability to keep me on the straight and narrow is beyond compare.

Thank you to our Head of Operations, Inclusion and Sustainability, Rachel. Since joining as an EA back in 2011 you've developed your skills to become a brilliant manager of our support team, you pretty much single-handedly got us our B Corp Certification in 2021 and your ability to calmly deal with every crazy idea we come up with amazes me every day.

Thank you to Leila and the fantastic Get Known team. As a first-time author I know I've been a royal pain in the derriere but your support through the process has been outstanding.

Of course, the final thank you has to go to Rowena and our amazing daughters, Charlotte and Hannah. It's no coincidence that my career took off after I met Row and to build our family together is the privilege of my life. So many stories written and so many more to come.